One Word From God Can Change Your Nation

Harrison House
Tulsa, Oklahoma

09 08 07 06 05 04 03 02 01 00   10 9 8 7 6 5 4 3 2 1

One Word From God Can Change Your Nation
ISBN 1-57794-200-0   30-0717
Copyright © 2000 by Kenneth Copeland Ministries
Fort Worth, Texas 76192-0001

Published by **Harrison House, Inc.**
P.O. Box 35035
Tulsa, Oklahoma 74153

Contents

Introduction

One Word From God Can Change Your Life FOREVER!

When the revelation of this statement exploded on the inside of me, it changed the way I think...about everything! I had been praying for several days about a situation that seemed at the time to be overwhelming. I had been confessing the Word of God over it, but that Word had begun to come out of my head and not my heart. I was pushing in my flesh for the circumstance to change. As I made my confession one more time, the Spirit of God seemed to say to me, *Why don't you be quiet?!*

I said, "But, Lord, I'm confessing the Word!"

He answered inside me, *I know it. I heard you. Now just be still and be quiet a little while, and let the Word of God settle down in your spirit. Quit trying to make this thing happen. You're not God. You're not going to be the one to make it happen anyway!*

So I stopped. I stopped thinking about that situation and began to get quiet before the Lord. And this phrase came up in my spirit: **"One word from God can change anything."**

So I started saying that. I said it off and on all day. It came easily because it came from God—not from my own thinking.

Every time I was tempted to worry or think of ideas concerning my circumstances, I'd think, *Yes, but one word from God...*

I noticed when I'd say that, **the peace of God** would come on me. It was so calming. As a result, a habit developed in me. People would bring me issues. They'd say, "Well, what about..." And I'd either say aloud or think to myself, **"Yeah, that may be so, but one word from God will change anything."**

It began to be the answer for everything. If I was watching television and the news-caster was telling about a disaster, and the people being interviewed were saying things to the effect of "Oh, what are we going to do? It's all been blown away, burned up or shook up...," I'd say, **"Yeah, but one word from God can change anything."**

It really developed into a strength for me, and it can for you too. That's why we've put together the *One Word From God* Book Series...there could be just one word in these inspiring articles that can change your nation forever.

You've been searching, seeking help... and God has the answer. He has the one word that can turn your circumstance around and put you on dry ground. He has the one word that gives you all the wisdom that's in Him. He is the King of kings and the Lord of lords. His Name shall endure forever, and men shall be blessed in Him. All nations shall call Him blessed (Psalm 72:17).

God loves you. And He has a word for you. One Word that can change your life FOREVER!

Kenneth Copeland

A Higher Form of Power

"The king's heart is in the hand of the Lord, as the rivers of water: he turneth it whithersoever he will."
— PROVERBS 21:1

Chapter 1

Kenneth
Copeland

What I have to say to you today is simple. And it is quite serious. Your response to it will not only affect your life and mine, but many thousands of others.

It is a message—no, a command—all of us have no doubt heard before. But by and large, we have ignored it. We have thought somehow we could get by without it, that we could let it slip without paying a price.

But we have paid. Our nations have paid. One look at any newspaper will give you an idea just how dearly.

The command I'm talking about is the one found in 1 Timothy 2:1-2. There the Apostle Paul says: *"I exhort therefore, that, first of all, supplications, prayers, intercessions, and giving of thanks, be made for all men; For kings, and for all that are in authority; that we may lead a quiet and peaceable life in all godliness and honesty."*

That verse is clear, isn't it? The instruction is plain. Yet even in these tumultuous days when our nations are so desperately in need of God's guidance, most of God's people don't do what that verse commands.

Why not?

Is it because we don't care? Is it because we're unwilling to invest a few minutes of prayer in the future of our nation each day?

No.

I believe it's because most of us are overwhelmed by the problems we see around us. *How could my prayers make a dent in the national debt?* we think. *How could my faith affect foreign policy?*

In other words, we fail to pray because we fail to realize just how powerfully our prayers can affect our countries.

So I want us to look at some scriptures and find out what the Word of God has to say about the subject.

First, let's look at Romans 13:1. There, the Apostle Paul writes: *"Let every soul be subject unto the higher powers. For there is no power but of God: the powers that be are ordained of God."*

It amazes me how little attention is paid to this very important scripture. In fact, when you get right down to it, most Christians don't even believe it! You can tell just by the disrespectful way they talk about their leaders.

"Well, if those leaders are ordained of God," you may say, "why don't they act like it?"

Because the believers they govern aren't praying for them!

You see, if by prayer we will invite God into our governments, He'll take control of those who've been put in positions of authority. As Proverbs 21:1 says: *"The king's heart is in the hand of the Lord, as the rivers of water: he turneth it whithersoever he will."*

Think about that for a moment! God has reserved the right to override the will of a nation's leader, if need be, to see that His people are governed according to His will.

What's more, God will hear the prayer of any government leader—even if he's the worst reprobate in the whole world. He heard the prayer of old King Nebuchadnezzar. And believe me, that means He'll listen to any leader!

When you have time, I encourage you to go to Daniel 4 and read the account of Nebuchadnezzar because it is a powerful example of what we're talking about here.

You see, Nebuchadnezzar was king of Babylon. He was an ungodly ruler of an ungodly nation. He had taken captives, however, from the land of Judah. He had some of God's people under his authority. So God began to deal with him.

Again and again, God warned him, "Nebuchadnezzar, you're going to lose your mind if you don't straighten up." But

Nebuchadnezzar refused to listen. And sure enough, he went just as crazy as could be.

He stayed that way for years too. Ran up and down through the woods like a wild man. Then one day he cried out to God and God heard him.

Despite his status as a heathen king of a heathen nation, God intervened repeatedly in Nebuchadnezzar's life and heard him when he finally cried out for help. Why? Because he had God's people under his control!

That same principle still holds true today. If we'll open the way through prayer, God will deal with our leaders! He'll turn the hearts of everyone from the top office on down to make sure His children are governed justly. In fact, if we'd just be obedient to 1 Timothy 2:1-2, there's no council of any kind on earth, no king, no president, no congress, not anyone who could overthrow God's purpose for His people.

The Constitution of the United States is a tremendous document, a Holy Ghost-anointed document in its original form. But, I'm telling you, it doesn't hold a candle to the Word of God. The Bible is heaven's constitution! And if we'll start believing it, praying it and acting on it where our nations are concerned, its power will whip our countries back into line with the will of God. And there won't be anything or anyone on earth that can stop it.

But if we're ever going to see that happen, we're going to have to take the Word of God and go to war in prayer and in faithful intercession. Unfortunately, most of us don't know the first thing about fighting such a war. For, as Ephesians 6:10-12 says, it's not a battle of flesh and blood, but of the spirit. In fact, let's look at those verses and see exactly what they say about this fight:

> **Finally, my brethren, be strong in the Lord, and in the power of his might. Put on the whole armour of God, that ye may be able to stand against the wiles of the devil. For we wrestle not against flesh and blood, but against principalities, against powers, against the rulers of the darkness of this world, against spiritual wickedness in high places.**

Read that last verse again. Most believers are so earthly minded (or carnally minded) they never even realize where the enemy's attacks are actually coming from. They blame circumstances and people, and they waste their energy fighting natural conditions instead of supernatural causes.

We need to wake up to the warfare that's going on in the heavenly realm!

We can get a glimpse of it in Daniel 10:12. There, we find Daniel had been fasting and praying for 21 days, awaiting a word from the Lord. Then an angel appeared to him and said: *"Fear not, Daniel: for from the first day that thou didst set thine heart to understand, and to chasten thyself before thy God, thy words were heard, and I am come for thy words."*

This angel had left heaven with the answer to Daniel's prayer on the first day he prayed. But he didn't arrive for 21 days. What took him so long?

Look at verse 13. *"But the prince of the kingdom of Persia withstood me one and twenty days: but, lo, Michael, one of the chief princes, came to help me; and I remained there with the kings of Persia."*

Then later in verse 20 he says, *"and now will I return to fight with the prince of Persia: and when I am gone forth, lo, the prince of Grecia shall come."*

These scriptures are clear examples of the activity and warfare going on in the heavens.

Sometimes when I talk about the warfare that takes place in the heavens, people get confused. "Heaven?" they say. "I thought the devil was thrown out of heaven."

What they don't realize is this: Throughout the Bible, we are taught there are three different areas called heaven:

1. **The heaven where God resides**

2. **The stellar heavens (what we call "outer space")**

3. **The heavens around this earth (the atmosphere surrounding this planet)**

This last heaven is where spiritual war takes place. (That's why Ephesians 2:2 calls Satan the prince of the power of the air.) It is where wicked spirits such as the prince of

Persia operate. From there, they attempt to rule the nations to which they've been assigned.

And they will rule them unless the prayers of God's people keep them from it.

Do you remember what Jesus said in Matthew 18:18? *"Whatsoever ye shall bind on earth shall be bound in heaven: and whatsoever ye shall loose on earth shall be loosed in heaven."*

The heaven Jesus was talking about there isn't the heaven where God resides. Nothing needs to be bound there. He was talking about the battle zone, about the heaven where Satan's forces are operating.

He was telling us we have been given the authority to pull down the strongholds of Satan (2 Corinthians 10:4). He was telling us God has given us the power to bind the wicked spirits in heavenly places and to loose the angelic powers of God to work on our behalf.

Jesus told Peter in Matthew 16:19: *"I will give unto thee the keys of the kingdom of heaven: and whatsoever thou shalt bind on earth shall be bound in heaven: and*

17

whatsoever thou shalt loose on earth shall be loosed in heaven."

The Greek text of that scripture would literally read, "I give you the keys of the kingdom. Whatever you declare locked on earth is locked in heaven and whatever you declare unlocked on earth is unlocked in the heavenlies."

Daniel couldn't do that. He didn't have the authority of the Name of Jesus. All he could do was hang on for 21 long, hard days until the angel of God could get through to him.

But praise God, you and I, as believers and as children of the Most High God, don't have to wait 21 days. We don't even have to wait 21 seconds for the angels to begin their work on our behalf!

Philippians 2:9-10 says we have been given a Name which is above every name, and at the Name of Jesus every knee shall bow in heaven, in earth and under the earth. That covers it all!

As believers, we have total authority over the powers of Satan. We can take authority over the evil spirits that are trying to destroy our nations. We can take authority over them in the Name of Jesus and pull down their strongholds.

It's time we began to realize how important we are to world affairs. Since the day Jesus gave us the Great Commission, the life or death of the world has been in the hands of the Church. We are the ones who have the mighty Name of Jesus and the awesome strength of the gospel to bring life and abundance to every creature. We are the ones whose prayers can change every office of authority in our lands.

Every few years, national elections take place in many nations. If we want nations of *"godliness and honesty,"* it's up to us to begin to intercede right now and use the power God has given us.

Right now, you need to be praying for all of the candidates. You need to find out who they are and then go to the Lord and ask which ones He's chosen. Don't just make your decisions by what the media says. Go to God. He knows the heart of each man and woman who's running for office. He'll give you supernatural guidance.

Be willing to set aside old ideas and past prejudices. I don't care if everybody in your family has voted Democratic ever since the Depression. I don't care if you've always voted a straight Republican ticket. If your country allows voting, vote Holy Ghost this time, OK? Vote however He says. (If you can't vote, you can still pray and have great effect.)

Did you notice what I just said? I said, VOTE.

The vote is a God-given privilege, a gift the Lord has given us. Don't throw it in His face by failing to take advantage of it!

In the last U.S. presidential election, there were millions of born-again, Holy Ghost-baptized, professing, believing Christians who weren't even registered to vote. Just think what a mighty army for God we would be if we all went to the polls during the next election. We could determine the outcome of elections with our votes if we only would.

God has called us to intercede. He has commanded us to pray for those in authority.

He has given us His Word, His power, His Name, His authority and His faith. We have all the tools necessary to pray effectively for our governments and their leaders.

Let's band together as never before in intercession for all the nations of the world. We are God's people, called by His Name, and we can stand in faith before Him for the healing of our lands.

Again, I urge you. If you haven't already registered to vote, do it today, right now. It is your responsibility as a believer to get involved in the affairs of your country. God wants these great lands of ours, and the only way He's going to get them is through His ambassadors—you and me.

If you've already registered, then come Election Day, make sure you go to the polls!

Don't let the affairs of your life sway you from the voting booth. And don't let anyone but the Holy Spirit tell you who you're to vote for. Start preparing yourself now by praying about the candidates and listening for the voice of the Lord.

God has an army marching in this earth. If we band together, we can prevent the wickedness in high places from ruling our nations. The time has come for us, as believers, to be counted both in prayer and at the polls. So let your voice be heard!

We may all come from different lands with different backgrounds, but we all have one thing in common—Jesus Christ is our Lord. And that alone is enough to alter the spiritual complexion of this earth.

How You Can Turn Your Nation to God

"When the righteous are in authority, the people rejoice: but when the wicked beareth rule, the people mourn."
— PROVERBS 29:2

Happy
Caldwell

What exalts a nation? What pulls it down? Do you know that people are confused on this subject? In the minds of many people it's the economy that lifts a nation up or pulls it down. Others think that the correct political party or the right elected officials will exalt a nation.

But God's Word says, *"Righteousness exalteth a nation: but sin is a reproach to any people"* (Proverbs 14:34). You can't fix a nation by just fixing its economy or by fixing its politics. You have to fix a nation by fixing its morality—by fixing its character and honesty.

Now there are many believers who understand this but are confused about God's righteousness and God's judgment. They think God is currently judging America, for example. But He's not. God is not judging America any more than He is judging Mexico or Guatemala or Italy or Africa.

God has already judged sin and Satan. If God was going to judge the homosexuals for their sin, then He'd have to judge drug addicts for their sin, alcoholics for their sin, and murderers for their sin. Is God a respecter of persons? No!

We don't live in the day of the vengeance of the Lord. Look carefully at where Jesus stopped reading Isaiah 61 that Sabbath day in the synagogue at Nazareth: *"The Spirit of the Lord is upon me, because he hath anointed me to preach the gospel to the poor; he hath sent me to heal the brokenhearted, to preach deliverance to the captives, and recovering of sight to the blind, to set at liberty them that are bruised, To preach the acceptable year of the Lord"* (Luke 4:18-19). Then He closed the book and sat down.

Jesus stopped in the middle of a sentence that went on to say *"and the day of vengeance of our God...."* (See Isaiah 61:2.) Why didn't

Jesus read all of it? Because the day of vengeance is coming, but it's not yet.

We are in the Church Age, the Age of Grace. This is not to say nations aren't inflicting all kinds of calamity upon themselves because of sin. Sin is a reproach to a nation, and a nation can be hurt by sin just as an individual can be hurt by sin. Sin carries with it the recompense of its reward.

But rather than see cities and nations continue in this kind of destruction, God has raised up believers who stand in the gap and intercede, just as Abraham stood up and did business for God at Sodom and Gomorrah. He said, *"Wilt thou also destroy the righteous with the wicked?"* (Genesis 18:23). No! Similarly, Jeremiah wept over Jerusalem as Jonah had Nineveh.

There have always been the revivalists, the intercessors, those that would stand between the porch and the altar and weep and cry out to God. There have always been the Charles Finneys, the Evan Robertses, the John G. Lakes and the Dwight L. Moodys whom God has used to stir nations. It has

25

always been the intercessors, not the politicians, who have changed the course of our nations.

What About My Nation?

Politics never has and never will change our nations. Men have tried it for years, and it's still not working.

God doesn't operate that way. He operates according to His Word.

God's plan is set forth in Proverbs 29:2: *"When the righteous are in authority [or leadership], the people rejoice: but when the wicked beareth rule, the people mourn."*

Notice that when the righteous are in authority, even the sinners will rejoice. They will rejoice, not *because* righteousness is increased, but *when* righteousness increases. Some of them won't know why, but they will rejoice because the righteous have increased in the earth. When righteousness is increased, God will exalt His nation and all citizens will live and enjoy the good life. (Read 1 Timothy 2:1-2.)

It should alarm us to hear people saying, "I don't care about character. I don't care about morality. I don't care about family. I don't care about whether the person is honest. All I care about is money, economics. What's going to put money in my pocket...How am I going to benefit from it...What am I going to get?" That's greed and materialism, and it will drive a country further into unrighteousness.

There is never a time or situation in the government of any nation in which character and morality *shouldn't* enter into a political contest. It's true that God is no respecter of persons. It's true that it rains on the just and the unjust alike. But it's the righteous who bring the rain and bring the blessings of God. It's the righteous who bring God in on the scene. "When the righteous are increased, the people rejoice." That is a spiritual principle. "When the wicked bear rule, the people mourn."

The Role of Intercession

What does it mean to bring righteousness on the scene? We are not talking about

27

a religion forcing everybody to go to church. God doesn't do that. Nor are we talking about self-righteousness. What we are talking about are two things you can do to change your nation and turn it around.

First, intercede in prayer for those who are in authority.

You may say, "I'm supposed to pray and intercede for all those who are in authority. What good is that going to do?"

One thing it will do is get you praying in line with God's will. First Timothy 2:1-4 says:

> I exhort therefore, that, first of all, supplications, prayers, intercessions, and giving of thanks, be made for all men; For kings, and for all that are in authority; that we may lead a quiet and peaceable life in all godliness and honesty. For this is good and acceptable in the sight of God our Saviour; Who will have all men to be saved, and to come unto the knowledge of the truth.

We went door-to-door during the National Evangelistic Census a few years ago. Out of all the houses my wife, Jeanne, and I went to, most of the people believed in God, but they didn't know how to pray. Because they didn't know how to pray, they didn't know whether they'd gotten a prayer answered or not.

During the census one man told us, "I believe in God, I believe in prayer and I believe I've gotten my prayers answered."

"Are you born again?" I asked.

"Oh, yes, I'm born again," he said.

"But you haven't had a life-changing experience with Jesus Christ?" I asked.

"No."

He didn't even know what a life-changing experience with Jesus Christ was... but he said he was born again.

Many of these people love God and they might even be born again, but they don't have the foggiest idea what I'm telling you right now. God's will for our nations is that men and women be saved and come to the knowledge of the truth so that they can pray in line with His will.

Do you want to get God involved in your prayers? Then make petitions, prayers, intercession and give thanks for all men. Intercede for all those in leadership who are in eminent places. This includes intercession for the president (or your prime minister, etc.), his cabinet and advisors, business-men, law enforcement officers, judges and congressmen. Pray for these people so that you may lead a quiet and peaceable life in all godliness and honesty. When you do, God will be involved with your prayers.

The Necessity of Involvement

Second, get involved politically and vote. If you don't vote and you are a Christian, then forget about praying. You are going to have to repent for sinning because you haven't taken advantage of your God-given, blood-bought right.

What most of the world is afraid of is Christians trying to force their values on everyone.

The head of the Arkansas Gay and Lesbian Task Force called me and asked if our church was going to get politically active.

"As individuals, yes, we always encourage people to get involved with politics and in the community," I said. "But as a church, we are called to preach the gospel, and that's what we are going to do. That's what we are here for. That's the assignment of the Church."

We are so shallow in our thinking. The issue is not the Democratic or the Republican Party—or any other party. The issue is righteousness. The issue is a spiritual issue. We must intercede for all men, kings, all that are in authority or all that are in an eminent or prominent place of leadership.

Why? It's simple. It's because God said if we will do this—and He exhorts us to do it—we will lead quiet and peaceable lives in all godliness and honesty. When righteousness increases and you have godly leadership, the people are going to rejoice. As we start interceding and petitioning for all men, the Holy Spirit starts to move, and people start getting saved, getting filled with the Holy Ghost and coming into the Church.

Then what happens? They go back into the workplace as saved people. Righteousness is increasing—right-standing with God, not self-righteousness, not holier-than-thou, not religious hypocrisy. People who are right with God are increased in the workplace.

This is exactly where Jesus told us we should go. Christians have stayed out of the marketplace when Jesus told us, *"Go ye into all the world"* (Mark 16:15). Christians should be witnesses everywhere we go. We should beget other Christians. As righteousness begins to increase, God will say, "Look at this; isn't this wonderful? Righteousness is increasing. It's time for us to exalt this nation, lift it up and bless it, because righteousness is increasing."

Then as the nation gets blessed, the people will be standing around and looking, saying "My, my, things sure are wonderful, aren't they? Crime's down, unemployment's down, wages are up, our environment is cleaned up, they're making progress on the national debt...." They start rejoicing. They start talking good. They start saying good things.

What's happening? God's doing what He said He'd do.

You can't fix a nation by just fixing its economy or its politics. You have to fix a nation by fixing its morality, its character, its honesty. When you do, then God gets involved in the nation.

God can solve the national debt problem, social injustice, unemployment, national health, environmental cleanup, and any other national challenge if we can just turn the nation around morally and see righteousness increase. When God gets involved, the people rejoice.

What we've looked for is for God to come in here and make everybody be a Christian. God has never done that, and He never will. We have to intercede. It's not an option anymore. But if you'll stand in the gap and intercede, God will move on your behalf and on behalf of your city, state, nation and world. Righteousness will exalt the nations.

Is Christ Divided?

Chapter 3

"And this gospel of the kingdom shall be preached in all the world for a witness unto all nations; and then shall the end come."
— MATTHEW 24:14

Creflo A. Dollar Jr.

Satan is in a last-days panic.

And in his fear and confusion he is using one of his number one weapons—the weapon of division. He's stirring up division and strife anywhere he can get people to agree with his deception. He's stirring it up in marriages, in homes, in churches, in businesses, among social classes and between ethnic groups.

In the United States, we've seen divorce rates soar. Order in the homes has almost disappeared. In recent years, the eyes of everyone have been riveted on racial division that has surrounded such events as the O.J. Simpson trial, the Million Man March and church burnings in the South. The races are sitting back waiting to see what is going to happen.

"Well, Pastor Dollar, what *is* going to happen?"

I know exactly what's going to happen. Jesus told us. In the midst of this situation, the glory of God is about to take off as it has never taken off before.

Yes, we are seeing evidence that the world is getting darker. We are seeing the signs of the devil's panic. He does not know quite how to respond because he's feeling the pressure. The end-time outpouring of God has begun and His glory is filling the earth. Jesus said:

> **And ye shall hear of wars and rumours of wars: see that ye be not troubled: for all these things must come to pass, but the end is not yet. For nation shall rise against nation, and kingdom against kingdom: and there shall be famines, and pestilences, and earthquakes, in divers places....But he that shall endure unto the end, the same shall be saved.**

And this gospel of the kingdom shall be preached in all the world for a witness unto all nations; and then shall the end come (Matthew 24:6-7, 13-14).

If you study the word "nation," you'll find it comes from the Greek word *ethnos*. We get our word *ethnic* from that. It means "a race, a tribe, an ethnic group."

Therefore, Jesus is saying that ethnic group shall arise against ethnic group and kingdom against kingdom. That's what we're seeing all over the earth today.

But notice that there is something else recorded in this passage. Believers are standing. They are resisting. They are refusing offense. They are not allowing the spirit of division to hold down the Body of Christ. They are preaching the gospel to all the world.

What's Really Scaring Satan?

What is Satan so afraid of? He's afraid of a powerful promise Jesus left to His followers: *"If two of you shall agree on earth as touching any thing that they shall ask, it shall be done for them of my Father which is in heaven. For where two or three are gathered together in my name, there am I in the midst of them"* (Matthew 18:19-20).

Satan knows what happens when believers multiply the power of their prayers through agreement.

In marriages, for instance, Peter tells husbands to honor their wives and treat them according to the knowledge of God's Word as *"heirs together of the grace of life"* so that their *"prayers be not hindered"* (1 Peter 3:7).

Walking in Unity

When two people start acting like one, they operate in a greater authority than they do by themselves. The devil knows that entire families walking together in unity can have everything the Bible says they can have, and there is nothing he can do about it. If one can put a thousand to flight, and two can put 10,000 to flight (Deuteronomy 32:30), imagine how much disarray a family of three, four or a dozen can bring to the enemy's forces!

They can lay hands on whomever outside the family needs ministry, because sickness won't come on those inside the family. They can walk in health and prosperity. And this can go from generation to generation. The devil doesn't have a chance with a family that's operating in oneness.

That's true for the Church, too. Churches come out of families.

Now we can understand why the devil tries to raise up differences between us to separate and divide us. In his letter to the church at Corinth, the Apostle Paul gives us a clear picture of how the spirit of division operates: *"For it hath been declared unto me of you, my brethren, by them which are of the house of Chloe, that there are contentions among you. Now this I say, that every one of you saith, I am of Paul; and I of Apollos; and I of Cephas; and I of Christ. Is Christ divided?"* (1 Corinthians 1:11-13).

I love his summary of the whole issue: *"Is Christ divided?"* Paul wrote that because separation is just the opposite of what Jesus came to give those who would believe in Him: *"As many of you as have been baptized into Christ have put on Christ. There is neither Jew nor Greek, there is neither bond nor free, there is neither male nor female: for ye are all one in Christ Jesus. And if ye be Christ's, then are ye Abraham's seed, and heirs according to the promise"* (Galatians 3:27-29).

Black or white, worker or boss, male or female, we all have the same rights and the same inheritance. We are children of Abraham by faith, and heirs of every promise and blessing of the Old Covenant and the New.

Designed for Differences

God's answer to differences is covenant. Covenant is designed for differences. It's designed to eliminate weaknesses. You might hear someone get up and say, "We are all alike." Folks, we are not all alike. We have some likenesses, but we are not all alike.

We have differences, and I appreciate our differences. It would be a boring world if we were all alike. Just imagine if all of us had the same name—Creflo! I'm glad we're different.

I didn't marry Taffi because she was just like me. I needed someone who was different than me. Where I am strong, she is weak. Where she is strong, I am weak. When people get married in covenant, they eliminate the weaknesses. They're not there anymore.

Not only does that take place in marriage, but it also takes place in business. Someone may be weak in the area of business and someone else might be strong. They come together in partnership and eliminate the weaknesses.

It's the same way with the Church. The black Church may be strong in one area, and the white Church may be strong in another. God hasn't designed us to stay apart. His best is that we come together in a covenant to eliminate the weaknesses. Recently, I was in a meeting where we started to sing praises, and all the white people started clapping on the downbeat and all the black people clapped on the upbeat. Whatever beat you wanted, we had it covered!

Covenant was not designed to get two families with the same strengths together. It was designed to match up one group's strengths with the other group's needs and weaknesses. It was designed to make one strong family out of two weak ones—each of them appreciating and drawing on the strengths of the other.

We've got a job to do, child of God. The solution for all division and strife is the gospel: *"And this gospel of the kingdom shall be preached in all the world for a witness unto all nations; and then shall the end come"* (Matthew 24:14).

When He was preparing His disciples for His return to the Father, Jesus declared, *"By this shall all men know that ye are my disciples, if ye have love one to another"* (John 13:35). Isaiah prophesied: *"Arise, shine; for thy light is come, and the glory of the Lord is risen upon thee. For, behold, the darkness shall cover the earth, and gross darkness the people: but the Lord shall arise upon thee, and his glory shall be seen upon thee. And the Gentiles shall come to thy light, and kings to the brightness of thy rising"* (Isaiah 60:1-3).

Nowhere to Come

The world won't have anywhere to come if we become just like them. We've got to be in a position to answer their questions when, after they've done everything, it doesn't make sense anymore. After trying everything they thought worked, the world is going to look at the Church and wonder why, when division is ripping loose every seam in the fabric of society, the Church is walking in love and unity and appreciation for differences. And we'll tell them, "Because we live according to the law of life in Christ Jesus which makes us free from the law of sin and death. We don't operate like you operate."

The gospel is the solution for every division. God has raised up men and women in every ethnic group in every nation to get it done. He has raised up men and women who are more concerned about your knowing Christ than what ethnic group you are from.

It is so important that we learn how to over-come and not let the spirit of division and separation come in.

There is a new breed of believers in the earth in these last days. It's a breed of covenant people who are not going to allow the spirit of division to invade our marriages, our homes, our countries or the Body of the Anointed One and His Anointing. It's a breed of believers who know the power of walking in oneness and want all of the glory in these last days.

The Anointing Can Change a Nation

"Now therefore ye are no more strangers and foreigners, but fellowcitizens with the saints, and of the household of God."
— EPHESIANS 2:19

Kenneth Copeland

In May of 1992, hopelessness hit the headlines. It grabbed the attention of the world as it drove angry, violent crowds into a destructive rage on the streets of South Central Los Angeles in the United States.

Businesses were burned. Stores were looted. Innocent bystanders were injured and even killed as people who felt trapped by circumstances, condemned to poverty and powerless over their own futures, erupted in frustration.

As the startling scenes reached into living rooms around the world by television, people began to ask, "What can we do? These people are hopeless! How can we change this situation?"

Some answered by calling for more government programs. Others cried out for financial aid. Still others called for more educational and employment opportunities. But I can show you by the Word of God that none of those things by themselves would have solved the situation. They wouldn't have gone to the source of the problem. In Ephesians 2:11-12, God reveals what that source is. Describing the condition all of us were in before we were born again, the Lord says: *"Wherefore remember, that ye being in time past Gentiles in the flesh...were without Christ, being aliens from the commonwealth of Israel, and strangers from the covenants of promise, having no hope, and without God in the world."*

According to the Word of God, hopelessness isn't caused by lack of money. It isn't caused by lack of education. It isn't caused by negative circumstances. Hopelessness comes from being without God in the world. It comes from being a stranger to His covenant.

Anybody anywhere can have hope if they know Jesus and the covenant promises of God. Your background, race or financial status doesn't matter. You can live in the worst ghetto in the world and still have hope in God because He isn't limited by man's resources. He isn't limited by man's prejudices. God is an equal opportunity employer!

Some people have said to me, "You ought not preach that prosperity message in poverty-stricken areas. You'll get those people's hopes up, and they don't have the same opportunity to prosper that you do."

Yes, they do!

I've seen God prosper people in places where there was absolutely nothing. No food. No jobs. No welfare program. Nothing! There is one country in Africa where the government wanted a tribe to die out, so they just stopped the flow of food and began to starve them to death. But that plan failed because some Holy Ghost-filled, African Christians refused to give up hope. They knew their covenant, so they prayed *"Give us this day our daily bread."* Do you know what happened? Those people got fed, and the government went under!

More Than Wishful Thinking

Understand this, though. When I say "hope," I'm not talking about the weak, wishful-thinking kind of attitude most people call hope. Real Bible hope isn't a wish. Hebrews 11:1 says, *"faith is the substance of things hoped for...."* There's no room for faith in wishing! For example, take the statement "I sure do wish God would bless me financially." There's no place in that statement for faith. It just won't plug in anywhere.

The Apostle Paul said in Philippians 1:20, *"According to my earnest expectation and my hope, that in nothing I shall be ashamed...."* If you'll look up the two Greek words translated "earnest expectation" and "hope," you'll find they're two different words that both mean the same thing. So hope *is* earnest expectation.

There's plenty of room for faith in earnest expectation. For instance, if you say, "I earnestly expect to receive financial blessings. I earnestly expect to be free from poverty." Faith can plug right into that statement. It just follows naturally. Faith becomes the substance of that statement.

Someone might ask, "How can you so intensely expect to prosper when the unemployment rate is up and the economy is down?" You can answer, "What I'm earnestly expecting isn't dependent on the world's economy. It's based on what God has promised in His covenant. Because He said it, I earnestly expect it!"

Can you hear the faith in those words? Certainly! Real Bible hope just opens the door so faith can walk right in!

Why don't we see more of that kind of hope in the Body of Christ? Because it is born out of the promises of God's covenant. And most Christians are using their believing faculties to believe some sort of religious system that men have designed instead of believing the Word of God. Despite the fact that they're born again with the seed of hope inside them, baptized in the Holy Spirit and walking around with a Bible tucked under their arm, they've become strangers to the covenants of promise.

You can tell those folks that 2 Corinthians 8:9 says Jesus became poor so we might be rich, and they'll answer, "Oh, yes, amen. I know it says that, Brother. But I just don't know whether to take the Bible literally or not."

The reason they don't know whether or not to take the Bible literally is because they're not spending any time in the Word as a covenant. That's what the word *testament* means. Did you know that? The New Testament is the New Covenant! It's not some kind of religious book. It is God's will and testament written down. It is a covenant of promise. It is God's blood-sworn oath.

I want you to imagine for a moment that you made a blood covenant with someone. You both cut your wrists, bound your hands together, mixed your blood and swore an oath to each other in your own blood. That would be serious, wouldn't it?

You know it would! But you have a covenant even more serious than that with Almighty God. It's a covenant ratified not by the tainted blood of a sinful man, but by the sinless blood of Jesus.

I've meditated on that fact until it's real to me. So when I pick up the New Testament, I'm not just reading a history book. I'm reading a copy of God's will and testament, and in my mind, I have Jesus by the hand and His blood is flowing down my wrist. Once you get a revelation like that, hope is no problem!

Figure in the Anointing

With those things in mind, let's go back to Ephesians 2 and dig a little deeper into what God is telling us about hope: *"For we are [God's] workmanship, created in Christ Jesus unto good works, which God hath before ordained that we should walk in them"* (verse 10).

Before we read any further, I want you to stop for a moment and notice the phrase *"created in Christ Jesus."* To truly under-stand that phrase, you need to realize that the word *Christ* is a Greek word. Why the English translators failed to translate it, I don't know. But that failure has cost us a great revelation.

You see, the word *Christ* isn't Jesus' last name. It's not a title. It's a word with a very significant meaning. *Christ* actually means "Anointed." *To anoint* is literally "to pour on, smear all over, or rub into." So the Anointing of God is to have God poured on, smeared all over and rubbed into.

Some time ago, the Spirit of God further clarified that definition for me. He said, *The Anointing of God is God on flesh doing those things only God can do.* Practically speaking, what does that Anointing of God on flesh do for us? According to Isaiah 10:27, it destroys the yoke of bondage.

Some people say the anointing breaks the yoke. But the word used in Isaiah isn't *break,* it is *destroy.* It literally means to obliterate so completely that there is no evidence the yoke ever even existed.

Now let's go back and read Ephesians 2, translating the word *Christ.*

Wherefore remember, that ye being in time past Gentiles in the flesh ...ye were without [the Anointed One], being aliens from the commonwealth

of Israel, and strangers from the covenants of promise, having no hope, and without God in the world: But now in [the Anointed] Jesus ye who sometimes were far off are made nigh by the blood of [the Anointed One] (verses 11-13).

According to those scriptures, before you were born again, you were without the Anointed One. Well, if you were without the Anointed One, you were also without the anointing, right? But now, you are in the Anointing of Jesus. That anointing is available to you in every situation to destroy (obliterate completely!) every yoke of bondage.

That's why you can have hope in the most hopeless situations. It doesn't matter who you are or what color your skin is. It doesn't matter if you never made it past the sixth grade. You can break out of that hopeless situation if you'll factor in the anointing.

The anointing factor is what the world always forgets. They say, "We'll build this wall so big nobody will ever get through it. We'll build it big enough to block out the gospel and keep the people under our thumb." But they fail to figure in the anointing factor. It will destroy that wall. If you don't believe it, ask the believers in Berlin!

I strongly suggest you begin factoring in the anointing in your life from this moment forward. If someone says, "Well, brother, you can't expect to succeed. You can't expect to prosper. You can't expect to get healed..." ask yourself, *Is there a yoke holding me back?* If the answer is yes, then rejoice because the anointing will destroy it!

"But Brother Copeland, I can't ever expect to get a good job because I can't read." Is that your yoke? Then believe God, and He'll destroy it.

I know a fellow who hadn't gone to school at all. God taught him how to read the Bible, but for a long time he couldn't read anything else. One day, he walked into the principal's office in the local high school and said, "I want to earn my diploma." The principal looked across his desk at this 40-year-old man and said, "OK, we can probably work something out. How much schooling have you had?"

"None," the man answered.

Shaking his head, the principal told him there just wasn't any way to overcome that kind of obstacle. But the man was persistent. "Now wait a minute," he said. "The Lord Jesus Christ has let me know that if I do my part and you do your part, He'll do His part. Yes, sir. There is a way."

Sure enough, in less than a year he had his high school diploma.

Don't Be a Stranger

Nothing is too big a problem when you figure in the anointing! So take hold of that anointing by beginning to expect. Start expecting something good to happen to you. Lay hold of the hope that's set before you in the promises of God.

Don't be a stranger to those promises. Dig into them, find out what God has said about your situation. Then start saying, "I expect it because God promised it!"

Think about that promise and meditate on it. Let it build an image inside you until you can see yourself well...until you can see yourself with your bills paid...until you can see yourself blessed and prosperous in every way.

If you'll do that, you'll eventually get bigger on the inside than you are on the outside. Your hope will grow so strong that the devil himself won't be able to beat it out of you.

Most believers never experience that kind of confident hope because they allow their emotions to pull them off course. They don't feel healed or they don't feel blessed, so they let the promises slip.

You can avoid that pitfall by anchoring your soul. Anchor it by becoming a follower of people like Abraham *"who through faith and patience inherit the promises."* (See Hebrews 6:11-20.)

The Bible says Abraham hoped against hope (Romans 4:18). He used the hope of the promise of God to fight against the natural "hope" (or hopelessness) that told him it would be impossible for Sarah and him to have a child.

Romans 4:21 says he was *"fully persuaded that, what [God] had promised, he was able also to perform."* Now, Abraham wasn't always fully persuaded. There was a time after God had promised to give him a child when he asked, "How can I know these things will happen?"

God answered him by cutting a covenant with him. Abraham killed the covenant sacrifice animals, split them down the center, laid the halves opposite each other and God walked in the blood of those animals. I believe with all my heart that Abraham saw God's footprints in that blood.

From then on, Abraham's soul was anchored. His mind couldn't argue with him. His emotions couldn't argue with him. His old, dead body couldn't argue with him. His barren wife couldn't argue with him. That covenant put an end to all arguments. From then on, Abraham was fully persuaded. Fully expectant.

Anchor Your Soul

God has made covenant with you just as surely as He made it with Abraham. But instead of making it in the blood and bodies of animals, He made it with the broken body and shed blood of His own Son, Jesus the Anointed One. That's what should be on your mind when you take Communion. Hebrews 6:17-19 says:

> **Wherein God, willing more abundantly to show unto the heirs of promise the immutability of his counsel, confirmed it by an oath: That by two immutable [unchangeable] things [the body and the blood of Jesus], in which it was impossible for God to lie, we might have a strong consolation, who have fled for refuge to lay hold upon the hope set before us: Which hope we have as an anchor of the soul, both sure and stedfast....**

Friend, we have hope because we're in blood covenant with Almighty God! Through Jesus we have access to Him. We *are no more strangers and foreigners, but fellow-citizens with the saints, and of the household of God!* (Ephesians 2:19).

When we're confronted by impossible situations in this world, we have a covenant right to factor in Jesus! Factor in the power of His Word! Factor in His Anointing!

Some say, "That sounds too easy." No, it's not easy! When the devil begins to tighten the noose of hopelessness around your neck with poverty or sickness or some other terrible situation, you have to fight and fight hard. Not by burning buildings and robbing stores—but by grabbing hold of the hope in the Word and using it to demolish every thought that would rise up against it.

"Casting down imaginations, and every high thing that exalteth itself against the knowledge of God, and bringing into captivity every thought to the obedience of Christ" (2 Corinthians 10:5).

The battleground where hope is won or lost is not on the streets, it's in the mind. It's in the imagination where expectancy begins to take form. So take your stand on that battleground. Begin now to expect the anointing to destroy the yokes in your life and in the life of your nation. Begin now to expect God to keep His covenant promises to you. Fight for that expectancy in the

Name of Jesus. Take your hope, fill it with faith and storm the gates of hell. They will not prevail against you or your country!

Chapter 5

Awake, O Sleeper!
The Dangers of Spiritual Drowsiness in the Last Days

Gloria Copeland

"Whatsoever is born of God overcometh the world: and this is the victory that overcometh the world, even our faith."
— 1 JOHN 5:4

We live in an evil day.

Actually, the days have been evil ever since Adam committed high treason in the Garden of Eden. But in this hour, that evil is intensifying because the end of the age is near. Jesus is coming soon, and the devil is doing everything he can to stop Him. He is killing, stealing and destroying as fiercely and rapidly as he can.

Never in my life have I seen a time when it was so absolutely necessary to walk continually before the Lord. Never have I seen a day when it was more crucial for us to heed the instructions God gives us in 1 Peter 5:8-9:

Be well-balanced—temperate, sober-minded; be vigilant and cautious at all times, for that enemy of yours, the devil, roams around like a lion roaring [in fierce hunger], seeking someone to seize upon and devour. Withstand him; be firm in faith [against his onset],—rooted, established, strong, immovable and determined—knowing that the same (identical) sufferings are appointed to your brotherhood (the whole body of Christians) throughout the world (AMP).

Look again at the first part of that verse. It says we must be vigilant. To be *vigilant* means to be "watchful and alert to danger." A *vigil* is "an act or time of keeping awake."

I've never seen a time when it has been more important to be awake spiritually, to be vigilant about the things of God, than it is right now. This is not the time for us to be lazy Christians. It's not the time for us to compromise in any area. This is the time for us to...

Take no part in and have no fellowship with the fruitless deeds and enterprises of darkness, but instead [let your lives be so in contrast as to] expose and reprove and convict them.... Awake, O sleeper, and arise from the dead, and Christ shall shine [make day dawn] upon you and give you light. Look carefully then how you walk! Live purposefully and worthily and accurately, not as the unwise and witless, but as wise— sensible, intelligent people; Making the very most of the time—buying up each opportunity—because the days are evil (Ephesians 5:11, 14-15, AMP).

As I was reading that scripture some time ago, that phrase *"Awake, O sleeper"* seemed to leap out at me. It reminded me that the "daily-ness" of life can sometimes lull us to sleep spiritually. It can cause us to doze off where the things of God are concerned. But I believe the Spirit of God is sending out a wake-up call to us today. He is saying, as He did through that verse in Ephesians, *Wake up, Sleeper! The day of the Lord is coming.*

What is it He is waking us up to, exactly? The three things that will take us through these evil, end-time days in strength and glory:

1. The Word of God

2. Prayer

3. The guidance of the Holy Spirit

No Time to Faint

Notice I listed the Word first. That's because the Word of God is your spiritual food. It generates faith—for as Romans 10:17 says, *"Faith cometh by hearing, and hearing by the word of God"*—and faith is what enables you to stand when the going gets tough.

Proverbs 24:10 says, *"If thou faint in the day of adversity, thy strength is small."* This is the day of adversity! You can't afford to be weak in this day and hour. You can't afford to faint spiritually in the trials of life. If you do, you'll be in trouble because, naturally speaking, things aren't going to get better in this world, they're going to get worse.

But don't let that scare you. For 1 John 5:4 tells us that *"whatsoever is born of God overcometh the world: and this is the victory that overcometh the world, even our faith."*

You can overcome every evil thing that comes against you if you'll just keep your faith strong. And the simple key to keeping your faith strong is this: Stay in the Word of God.

Did you know you can become just as strong as you want to from the Word? The only limiter is you. If you'll give the Word more time, it will give you more strength.

That's what wise believers do. They keep themselves strong by spending time in the Word every day. They stay strong and ready because they know this is an evil day we live in.

Wake yourself up to the Word by getting out your Bible and meditating on it every day. Get tapes and books of anointed men and women preaching the Word. Listen to them and read them again and again.

Keep that Word in your heart. Keep it going in your eyes and in your ears until it takes over the very thoughts that you think. That's the first key to overcoming in this dangerous day.

No Voice Mail in the Throne Room

The second key is found in Romans 12:12, *"Be constant in prayer"* (AMP).

James 5:13 says, *"Is any among you afflicted [or in trouble]? let him pray...."*

Notice that verse doesn't say, "If anyone is in trouble, he should ask his pastor to pray." No, it says if there is trouble in your life, you need to pray.

It's wonderful to have a good pastor and know people who can pray with power—and I certainly ask for prayer from others when I need it—but it's *your* prayers that are most important.

That's because prayer is more than just asking for something. When you pray, you fellowship with your Father. You talk to Him. He talks to you. As a result, not only are your requests answered—you are strengthened through that interaction with Him.

I was reminded of that recently at a family gathering. One of our family members had gone home to be with the Lord unexpectedly, and it was a challenging time. After we had shared together and praised the Lord, one of my cousins came up to me and said, "It just strengthens my faith to be around this family."

I knew exactly what she meant. I know people who are more mature in faith and have been walking with the Lord longer than I have. And when I fellowship with those people, it makes me stronger too.

As I thought about that, it dawned on me—if a person who is full of faith can strengthen me, how much more does it strengthen me to fellowship with God Himself every day in prayer? Think about that!

You have the privilege any time of the day or night to draw near to God Himself and come into His presence. You can keep a running dialogue going with the Lord all day long. You can be constant in prayer, continually drawing strength from the Author and Finisher of your faith.

He is always ready to listen and respond to you.

That's not true of anyone else. Sometimes, for example, I'll call my own office and get what we call voice mail on the line. A recording will say, "I'm out right now, but your call is important to me. Please leave a message."

But you never get voice mail when you talk to God. Never! At 3 o'clock in the morning, He is right there, ready to visit with you. In fact, He sent His Spirit to live in you so He could communicate with you every moment of the day.

If you haven't already done so, it's time you woke up to that fact and started taking advantage of it! It's time you set aside special time to pray and commune with God every day.

I'll never forget when I first began to do that. It was after I heard a prophecy given by Brother Kenneth Hagin in 1982. In that prophecy, he said:

Don't take up all your time with natural things—some of those things are legitimate and it's all right to take a certain period of time there—but see to it that you give heed (watch, listen to, pay attention) unto your spirit and you give your spirit opportunity to feed upon the Word of God and you give your spirit opportunity to commune with the Father....It doesn't take a lot of time, just an hour or two out of 24; just pay a tithe of your time unto Me, saith the Lord, and all will be well. Your life will be changed. It will be empowered, and you will be a mighty force for God.

That word became a word from heaven to me more than 15 years ago, and I began to set aside time every morning to pray.

At that time, John was just a young teenager and I was concerned about him. He wasn't a bad boy; he just wasn't doing the things I knew he should do. That word from the Lord said to me that if I'd spend an hour or two in fellowship with Him

69

each day, all would be well. I acted on it, and it came to pass in my life.

You know, just an hour or two a day is not very much to invest in order to have everything in your life be well. And I can vouch for the fact that it really works, because today all is well in our lives. All our children, including John, are dedicated to the Lord and serving Him with us in ministry.

Listen and Obey Your Instructions

I believe the Holy Spirit quickened that prophecy to me because He wanted to prepare me for things to come. He was endeavoring to guide me and my family safely around the traps and pitfalls the devil had laid for us.

When the man of God spoke from heaven it was not just to me, but to the Church.

He wants to do the same for you and every other member of the Body of Christ. That's why it's so vital that we wake up to His voice!

Right now, more than ever before, it's crucial for us to tune in to those small promptings in our spirit—and to obey them. When the Lord says to you, for example, *Don't spend so much time playing golf, or talking on the phone or watching television right now. Give yourself to spiritual things instead,* don't try to figure out why; just be obedient.

There's always a reason for His instructions. I found that out myself not long ago.

Ken and I were on vacation at the time. We were just relaxing and enjoying ourselves when, suddenly, the Lord began impressing me not to watch any more secular television and to spend my time saturating myself with the Word of God instead.

I didn't particularly want to hear that instruction. After all, I was on vacation! But He continued to prompt me about it, so I got busy. I turned off the television completely and began listening to tapes and studying the Word throughout the day.

Looking back now, I'm so glad I did that, because I was about to be faced with a situation so serious that it would demand great spiritual strength for me to face it and overcome. The Lord wasn't just trying to interrupt my vacation. He wanted to strengthen me with His might so I'd be prepared for the trouble ahead.

Can you see why it's so vital that we listen to the voice of the Spirit in this day? Can you see why we must hear what He is saying to us and quickly obey? It's because He is giving us the instructions we need to live in victory 24 hours a day, every day of the year!

Blaze a Path

Listen, the world around us really is getting darker in these last days, and to walk through that darkness in triumph is definitely no stroll in the park. But we can do it if we'll just be vigilant and alert to the dangers.

We can do it if we'll obey the instructions God gives us in Romans 12:21 and *"Be not overcome of evil, but overcome evil with good."* After all, God has given us so many good things, so much supernatural power and ability, that no matter what happens in this dark world, we can emerge from it a winner. He has given us weapons of warfare that are not carnal, *"but mighty through God to the pulling down of strong holds"* (2 Corinthians 10:4).

In fact, if we'll shake off the sleepiness of daily living and start walking in the spirit, we can blaze a path through it a mile wide. We can not only make it through this shadowy place to the light of glory; we can take millions of others with us!

We can put hell itself on the run if we'll just wake up! Wake up to the Word of God. Wake up to prayer. Wake up to the guidance of the Holy Spirit. For in those things, God has given us all the power, strength and wisdom we need to overcome!

Chapter 6

The Might and Ministry of the Holy Spirit in You

"The Lord is high above all nations, and his glory above the heavens."

— PSALM 113:4

Kenneth Copeland

Believers today have vastly underestimated the power of the Holy Spirit.

You may wonder how I can be so sure of that. It's simple, really. If we truly understood and believed what the Bible tells us about Him, we would never worry about anything again. All hell has to offer could come against us and we wouldn't fear. We'd just grin and say, "Bring it on, devil! The Greater One lives within me, and He has given me all the wisdom, strength, power and provision I need to crush you like a bug."

Right now you may think you could never have that kind of boldness. But let me ask you something: What would you do if Jesus appeared to you today? How would you act if He linked His arm in yours and told you that from now on, He would be physically present with you in every situation. If you became sick, He would lay His hand on you and you'd be healed. If you ran short of money, He'd pray and multiply your resources. If you encountered a problem you didn't know how to handle, He'd tell you exactly what to do.

Under those circumstances, you'd be very bold and confident, wouldn't you? Every time you ran into trouble, you'd just glance over at Jesus standing next to you and suddenly you'd have great courage.

Of course, there's one problem. The fact is, you don't have that advantage. You don't have Jesus standing next to you in the flesh taking care of your every need.

But you do have something better.

I realize it's difficult to believe there's anything more beneficial than Jesus' physical presence. But there is. Jesus said so Himself.

That's right. In the hours just before He was crucified, He told His disciples that He would be leaving them and returning to His Father in heaven. When they expressed their sorrow and dismay, He said:

> I will pray the Father, and he shall give you another Comforter, that he may abide with you for ever; Even the Spirit of truth; whom the world cannot receive, because it seeth him not, neither knoweth him: but ye know him; for he dwelleth with you, and shall be in you.... I tell you the truth; It is expedient for you that I go away: for if I go not away, the Comforter will not come unto you; but if I depart, I will send him unto you (John 14:16-17, 16:7).

To fully grasp the impact of this last statement, you have to realize that Jesus was talking to a group of men who had followed Him day and night for three years. They had seen His miracles. They had enjoyed perfect protection and provision at His hand.

Peter was sitting there among them. Can't you just imagine what was running through his mind? No doubt he was thinking of the

ONE WORD FROM GOD CAN CHANGE YOUR NATION

first time Jesus had borrowed his boat. After He'd finished preaching from it, He'd said to Peter, "Grab your nets and we'll go catch us some fish." It was the middle of the day. Peter knew you couldn't catch fish in the daylight in that lake—the water was too clear. The fish would see the net and run from it.

But just to humor Him, Peter had done what Jesus said and ended up with a net-busting, boat-sinking load of fish. What a day!

Then there was the time Jesus healed Peter's mother-in-law of a deadly fever. Cured her instantly!

Even that didn't hold a candle to what happened on the Mount of Transfiguration. That day, Peter had actually seen Moses and Elijah talking with Jesus. He had watched His body transfigure before his very eyes. He'd seen the shining cloud of glory and heard the awesome voice of Almighty God!

As those events passed through Peter's mind, he must have wondered, *How can it possibly be expedient, or to my advantage, for Jesus to go away?*

Knowing that question was in the heart of every one of His disciples, Jesus said, in essence, "I know this is hard for you to believe, but trust Me on this. I'm not lying to you. It's better for you if I go away so that I can send the Holy Spirit to not only be with you, but to be in you!"

The Muscle of God

It's been almost 2,000 years since Jesus said that, and most of us are still struggling to fully believe it.

Theologically, we know it's true, and we thank God that we're born again and baptized in the Holy Ghost. But then we open our mouths and say things like, "If I could just feel Jesus' hand on my fevered brow, it would be easier for me to receive my healing."

Why is that?

I believe it's because we haven't truly appreciated the might and the ministry of the

Holy Spirit. We haven't yet had a full revelation of Who this is that is living inside us.

Many Christians, for example, seem to think the first time the Holy Spirit did much of anything was on the Day of Pentecost. But that's not true. The Holy Spirit has been at work on this planet ever since the beginning. Look at the book of Genesis and you can see that for yourself. There in the first few verses we find: *"In the beginning God created the heaven and the earth. And the earth was without form, and void; and darkness was upon the face of the deep. And the spirit of God moved upon the face of the waters. And God said, Let there be light: and there was light"* (Genesis 1:1-3).

Think about that! The Holy Spirit was hovering, waiting to create. Then the moment God spoke the Word, "Light be!" (literal Hebrew translation), the Spirit sprang into action and slung this universe into being.

That's how the Bible introduces us to the Holy Spirit!

You see, the Holy Spirit is the muscle of God. Every time you see God's power in manifestation, you can be sure the Holy Spirit is on the scene.

When the Holy Spirit came on Samson, he single-handedly killed a thousand Philistine soldiers. (See Judges 15:14-16.) Can you imagine how embarrassing that must have been for the Philistines who escaped? They probably went running back to headquarters all beat up and breathless with the story of this terrible massacre. I can almost hear their commander's response.

"A thousand men killed? A thousand? That's awful! How many Israelites were you up against?"

"Uh, well, sir...actually, just one."

Some people get the idea that Samson was able to do those great exploits because he was a giant of a man. But he was really just an ordinary fellow. He only became extraordinary when the Spirit of God came on him.

The prophet Elijah was the same way. On his own, he was just as normal as you and me. He was once so frightened by the threats of a woman that he hid in the wilderness and asked God to kill him so he wouldn't have to face her.

But when the Holy Spirit came on him, Elijah was a powerhouse. He once called down fire from heaven, killed 400 prophets of Baal, and outran the king's chariot (drawn, no doubt, by the fastest horses in the nation of Israel). And he did it all in one day. (See 1 Kings 18-19.)

What a Mind!

Don't get the idea from those examples, however, that the Holy Spirit is simply a mindless source of raw power. Far from it! When He moves in on a situation, He does it with wisdom and understanding so vast that it staggers the human mind.

Isaiah 40:13 says of Him: *"Who hath directed the spirit of the Lord, or being his counsellor hath taught him?"* Now go back and read how verse 12 further explains: *"Who hath measured the waters in the hollow of his hand, and meted out heaven with the span, and comprehended the dust of the earth in a measure, and weighed the mountains in scales, and the hills in a balance?"*

Consider for a moment what kind of mind could take a handful of water, weigh it and then compute all the moisture changes of the earth that would take place over untold thousands of years. What kind of mind could take a handful of dust, weigh it, and then figure out how to form the earth— mountains and all—in such a way that it would always stay in perfect balance?

That's the kind of mind the Spirit of God has!

When He put this earth together, He did it so perfectly that it can travel 1,000 miles an hour in one direction and 10,000 miles an hour in another, both at the same time, without ever getting the slightest degree off course. He constructed it so that it could compensate for all the movement of the tides and all the use and abuse it would receive at the hands of man and still make its way through the heavens exactly on time.

Listen, He is the One Who is planning your life! He is the One Who dwells within you and walks within you. When you join yourself to the Lord, you become one spirit with Him (1 Corinthians 6:17). And He didn't change or shrink up His abilities so He could fit them inside you.

No, if you're a born-again, Holy Spirit-baptized believer, He is everything in you that He has ever been. He has the same awesome power. He has the same astounding ability to compute, comprehend and plan in infinite detail everything that has ever been...everything that now is...and everything that ever will be!

What's more, when you run into something you can't handle and you call on Him for help, He's not a million light years away. He's right there inside you! He's ready to supply you with whatever you need. He's ready to be your Comforter. Ready to be your Teacher and your Trainer. Ready to be your Advocate, your Standby, your Counselor. He's ready to put His supernatural muscle and mind to work for you 24 hours a day.

The Perfect Gentleman

"Well then, why hasn't He helped me before now?" you ask. "Heaven knows I've needed it!"

He's been waiting for you to give Him something He can work with. He's been waiting there inside you just as He hovered over the face of the waters in Genesis, waiting for you to speak the Word of God in faith.

That's been His role since the beginning—to move on God's Word and deliver the power necessary to cause that Word to manifest in the earth. That's what He did at creation...and that's what He is commissioned to do for you.

But remember, He's your Helper, not your dominator. If you're walking around talking doubt, unbelief and other worthless junk, He is severely limited. He won't slap His hand over your mouth and say, "You dummy, I don't care what you say; I'm going to bless you anyway."

No, the Holy Spirit is the perfect gentleman. He'll never force anything on

85

you. He'll just wait quietly for you to open the door for Him to work.

So decide right now to start opening that door. Develop an awareness of the reality of the Holy Spirit within you. Stop spending all your time meditating on the problems you're facing and start spending it meditating on the power of the One inside you Who can solve the problems. In other words, start becoming more God-inside minded!

Do you know what will happen if you do that? All heaven will break loose in your life.

Instead of walking around moaning about how broke you are and how you can't afford to give much to spread the gospel, you'll start thinking about the fact that the One with the power to bring God's Word to pass is living inside you, and you'll change your tune. You'll start saying things like, "God meets my needs according to His riches in glory, so I have plenty to meet my own needs and give to every good work!"

Then the Holy Spirit within you will go into action. He'll give you plans, ideas and inventions. He'll open doors of opportunity and then give you the strength and ability to walk through them.

Instead of sitting around wishing there was something you could do for your sick, unsaved neighbor, you'll march into his house, tell him about Jesus, and then lay hands on him, fully expecting the Holy Spirit within you to release God's healing power and cause him to recover.

Instead of sitting around simply admiring the works of Jesus and reading about them each Sunday in church, you'll hit the streets and do those works yourself—and even greater works. (See John 14:12.) You'll stand up boldly and say:

> **The Spirit of the Lord is upon me, because he hath anointed me to preach the gospel to the poor; he hath sent me to heal the brokenhearted, to preach deliverance to the captives, and recovering of sight to the blind, to set at liberty them that are bruised, To preach the acceptable year of the Lord (Luke 4:18-19).**

87

More Than You Can Think

"Wait a minute, Brother Copeland. Jesus spoke those words about Himself!"

Yes, He did. But He also said, *"As my Father hath sent me, even so send I you"* (John 20:21).

You've been sent just as Jesus was. You've been sent to your family, your neighborhood, your workplace, your nation, your world to deliver the burden-removing, yoke-destroying power of God!

That's the reason God baptized you in the Holy Spirit. He intended for you to walk into a place and bring the power of God on the scene—the same power that enabled Samson to defeat the Philistines and make a fool out of the devil! The same power that enabled Elijah to call down fire from heaven and outrun the fastest horses in the country! The same power that enabled Jesus to heal the sick, raise the dead and calm the sea!

Can you imagine what all God could do in this earth if we'd just become God-inside minded enough to let that power flow?

No, you can't. For as the Apostle Paul said, He is *"able to do exceeding abundantly above all that we ask or think, according to the power that worketh in us"* (Ephesians 3:20).

Maybe you've been waiting for God to do something in your life or in the lives of those around you. Maybe you've been saying, "I know God is able to change this situation. I wonder why He doesn't do it?" If so, read that last phrase again. It says He is able to do above what we can ask or think according to the power that worketh in *you!*

Start building your faith in that power. Instead of always gazing toward heaven saying, "God, why don't You help me?" look at yourself in the mirror and say, "The Spirit of God is living in me today, and I expect Him to do wise, wonderful, amazing and miraculous things through me!"

Instead of meditating on your problems and natural inadequacies, get out your Bible and study the acts of the Holy Spirit from Genesis to Revelation. Start meditating on the power and sufficiency of the

Greater One Who lives and walks within you every moment of every day.

When you begin to realize what a dynamite team you two really are, you'll blast off into the realm of exceedingly above all that you can ask or think...and the devil will never be able to catch you.

People of Principle

"Arise, shine; for thy light is come, and the glory of the Lord is risen upon thee. For, behold, the darkness shall cover the earth, and gross darkness the people: but the Lord shall arise upon thee, and his glory shall be seen upon thee."

— ISAIAH 60:1-2

Happy Caldwell

When the United States' founding fathers walked out of Constitution Hall, they asked Ben Franklin, "What do we have, a democracy or republic?" He answered, "You have a republic...if you can keep it."

America is a republic, or at least that's what it was set up to be. Yet many people mistakenly think it is—and was meant to be—a democracy. But it's not, though it's slowly becoming one.

The difference is, a republic is ruled by law, not people. A democracy, on the other hand, is ruled by a majority of people. In a democracy, all it takes is for the wrong majority of people to rule and you've got trouble.

America was created to be a nation governed by law. And those who were elected and appointed to positions of authority were expected to follow that law—that is, the Constitution of the United States. The danger is, when people of a republic cease to be people of principle, they stop following the law. As a result, the republic can be lost.

Today, America faces that danger.

Decades of Decline

I was born during World War II and grew up in postwar America. In those days, the nation was growing, the economy was growing, yet people still cared about each other. There was morality.

But then came the '60s. It was like day and night.

After I came home from serving in the Navy and sailing around the world, I sensed a difference. The people in my hometown had changed. But that wasn't all—prayer had been taken out of the schools. When I had attended school, teachers led prayer every day. No one would have ever thought a day was coming when children could no longer pray in their classrooms.

Many sudden changes happened in this country, and with the '70s came more. That's when we licensed doctors to kill unborn babies by abortion. And another holocaust of life started.

Then, there were the '80s. They brought a different kind of change. A slight trend surfaced countering the radical changes of the previous 20 years.

Now, here we are marching into the 21st century.

I have watched 50 years come and go, and from what I see today, we really do live in a different time—a time of moral and social decline. Having seen this decline firsthand, I recently began asking myself— and the Lord—*What caused it? Why all this change in America?*

Of course, it would be easy to say, "Well, it's the devil. Satan is behind it all."

But a blanket statement like that does not cover the whole truth of the matter. It's not just the devil.

As I considered what could have given ground to the downward changes I've seen in our society, I suddenly realized the answer: People of principle.

Certainly Satan has eroded the foundations of our society, but only because we—America—are no longer a people of principle. Even more seriously, however, we as believers have not been people of principle... people of God's principles.

This isn't the first time God's people have witnessed—and been a part of—a moral decline due to a lack of principle.

Back to Boot Camp

In dealing with the moral decline of certain New Testament churches, the Apostle Paul also saw the lack of God's principles in Christians' lives as the root to their problems. He had this to say to them: *"For when for the time ye ought to be teachers, ye*

*have need that one teach you again which
be the first principles of the oracles of God;
and are become such as have need of milk,
and not of strong meat"* (Hebrews 5:12).

These Christians had started off with a
good foundation. But what happened?

They slipped into carnal and immature
ways.

Then along came Paul to build on their
foundation, only to find that it wasn't
there anymore.

This was a man who had life-changing,
empowering revelations about the mysteries of God to pass along. But instead of
being able to give them strong meat to
chew on, he had to spoon-feed them the
milk of the Word. He had to go back to the
basics of faith—repentance from dead works,
baptism, laying on of hands, etc.

And that's what has happened to the
Church today. We are not receiving revelation of the gospel's mysteries because we do
not know—and have not continued in—the
basic, foundation principles of God's Word.

Paul went on to say: *"Therefore leaving the principles of the doctrine of Christ, let us go on unto perfection"* (Hebrews 6:1).

Once we lay these principles of God in our hearts, we need to go on—that is—we need to build on them. But leaving these principles, as Paul said, doesn't mean we don't need them anymore.

When you build the foundation of a house, you don't stop there; you add to it. You put up walls and a roof and finish it out.

And after building the house, you don't decide, "Well, let's go pull out the foundation. We're through, so we won't need it anymore." The whole house would fall apart if you did—which is the very reason America is caving in. Our foundation is slowly being pulled out from under us.

We cannot let go of God's principles and stand. Principles like faith, repentance and righteousness are what we build our new lives on. They are part of our lifestyle. We must lay them up in our hearts. Once we do, it's time to build on them.

To better understand what this nation—and the Body of Christ—is lacking, let's turn to God's Word and study an example of the finished product. Let's see how God describes a person of principle.

Abraham—A Man of Principle

In Genesis 18, God makes some powerful statements about Abraham, the greatest of which is, *"I know him..."* (verse 19).

Keep in mind that Abraham was a man with whom God personally shared important information, events of the future, and upon whom He was able to build nations. God knew Abraham and trusted him.

In verse 19, God goes on to describe Abraham by listing three characteristics that distinguish him as a man of principle.

First, God says Abraham is one who *"will command his children and his household after him...."*

Now that doesn't mean he's a dictator, ruling with a heavy hand. Rather, it means he takes responsibility for his children.

Many of our nation's problems exist because parents are not commanding their children. They are not taking authority or being responsible for them.

In particular, fathers have shirked their responsibility to the point where laws have been passed to make them take care of their children—even to feed and clothe them. It's hard to imagine a father not wanting to care for his children, but because we are no longer people of principle, we now rely on laws to force them to fulfill their responsibility.

God says about Abraham, *"He will command his children and his household after him, and they shall keep the way of the Lord"* (verse 19).

The second characteristic of Abraham that distinguished him as a man of principle was that he was an example for his family to follow.

A father's responsibility includes setting that example—it's not the pastor's, not the athlete's, not the movie star's. It's the father's. Father should know best—and live it. When I was growing up, he did. Now, he's portrayed as a fool, a bungling idiot. Watch most TV depictions of a father and you'll see a man who can't make decisions. He's continually made fun of by everyone.

So it's not enough for you to command your children—to be their authority—you also need to be their model. Whether you're a parent or not, you should be a good example to your household and community.

I know you parents have plenty of pressure on you to give in and not stand up as people of principle. Everything in the world is pulling on you. Even your family pulls on you to compromise at times...

"Oh, do we really have to go to church today? Why can't we...."

But if you don't remain a steadfast person of principle, you'll get watered down, you'll start letting things slide, and before you know it, you'll have lost your standard of God's principles.

Meanwhile, your family is watching and they too begin losing their principles. Eventually, the next generation is raised without principles, and moral decline takes over.... Have you seen the bumper sticker, "If it feels good, do it"?

Finally in verse 19, God says Abraham *"will command his children and his household after him, and they shall keep the way of the Lord, to do justice and judgment...."*

Justice means "rightness" or "moral virtue." Plug that into this scripture and it reads, "Abraham will teach his household rightness and moral virtue."

Being a person of principle can be like paddling a boat upstream—it can get pretty tough. While everyone else is drifting lazily downstream, you need power and life to go against the flow. You need strength to follow rightness and moral virtue.

Judgment means "verdict, a sentence or decree, and the penalty that suits a crime."

In my home state, at last count, I heard there were 15 prisoners on death row. And some of them have been there more than 10 years.

So why haven't they been executed? The reason is the appeal system—it tends to drag on and on, which creates a problem.

There is a law of nature that says for every action, there is an equal and opposite reaction. Apply that to our judicial system and you can see that because the judgment isn't carried out, we have to build bigger jails to house more and more criminals. To criminals, the judicial system is a joke, so they keep on breaking the law.

Some people say that proves the death penalty is not a deterrent to crime.

Not true!

The truth is, punishment for crime has been diminished to almost nothing, and the result has been that the foundation of judgment has slowly crumbled, giving way to moral and social decline.

Though I have seen more than 30 years of moral decline in America, I still believe there is hope to turn this country around. How?

Declaration of Principle

Consider this question: Why was it so important for God to find a man like Abraham, a man who would command his children, a man who would set the example for others to follow, and a man who would do justice and judgment—a man of principle?

Read God's final comments about Abraham in Genesis 18:19 and you'll see why. You'll also see the hope there is for America. *"so the Lord may bring Abraham what He has promised him"* (AMP).

God was looking for a man to bless. But God can only bless those who build and live their lives on His principles—on His Word.

America was once a nation of people who built their lives on God's principles. But as we have ceased to be people of principle, as the Church has ceased to be established on God's principles, we have, in effect, tied God's hands to where He cannot bring to pass in our lives and in this nation all that He has promised.

How can we even begin to turn around a nation that has been declining for decades?

Let's look to the Middle East for a moment and consider another "impossible" situation—peace.

A few years ago the world watched as nations of the Middle East worked toward peace. But those peace efforts really began months earlier with the Israeli-Palestinian Declaration of Principle.

Now this declaration wasn't a peace treaty. It was only the beginning.

The peace effort started as heads of state came together, sat down and actually declared the principles by which they would negotiate peace. This was their foundation upon which to build peace. Meanwhile, however, the people of their countries were still in the streets fighting and killing each other.

If we as believers want all of God's blessings in our homes, in our businesses and in our nations, then we must begin by declaring God's principles and living them—in our churches, classrooms and public offices.

Then, we must build on that foundation. As Paul wrote in 2 Timothy 3:14-15: *"But you must continue in the things which you have learned and been assured of, knowing from whom you have learned them, and that from childhood you have known the Holy Scriptures"* (NKJV).

I have lived long enough to see a generation change. Sadly, though, the change has been for the worse. Yet, in my lifetime, I have seen that people of principle never change...because the principles of God never change.

Chapter 8

The Power of Consecration to Principle

John G. Lake

"Blessed are the poor in spirit: for theirs is the kingdom of heaven."
— MATTHEW 5:3

The great purpose of Jesus Christ's coming to the world was to establish the kingdom of God. The kingdom of God is universal, containing all moral intelligences, willingly subject to the will of God, both in heaven and on earth, both angels and men. The kingdom of heaven is Christ's kingdom on the earth, which will eventually merge into the kingdom of God. We read of that merging period in 1 Corinthians 15, where it says:

> Then cometh the end, when he shall have delivered up the kingdom to God, even the Father; when he shall have put down all rule and all authority and power...And when all things shall be subdued unto

him, then shall the Son also himself be subject unto him that put all things under him, that God may be all in all (verses 24, 28).

Now then, in order to establish a kingdom, there must be a basis upon which it is to be founded. When the Revolutionary fathers got together in '76, they laid down the Declaration of Independence—the principles upon which American government was to be founded. They laid down as one of the first principles this one: "All men are born free and equal"—That every man, by his being born a man, is likewise born on an equality with all others. All men are born free and equal before the law; there is no special privilege.

Next, they considered this as the second principle: Man, because of his birth and his free agency, is entitled to "Life, liberty, and the pursuit of happiness."

Third: Government rests on the consent of the governed.

These were the underlying principles upon which the government was to rest.

There was nothing little about them. They did not discuss the doctrines by which these principles were to be made effective, but they laid down the foundational principles upon which was built the greatest system of human government in the world's history.

Likewise, Jesus, when He came to found His kingdom, first enunciated the principles upon which His government was to rest. The eight Beatitudes, as they are given in His official declaration in His Sermon on the Mount, were the great principles upon which His government was to be founded.

A principle is not a dogma or a doctrine. It is that underlying quality, that fundamental truth, upon which all other things are based; and the principles of the kingdom of heaven are those underlying qualities upon which the whole structure of the Christian life rests, and the principles upon which the real government of Jesus Christ will be founded and exercised. The eight Beatitudes are the principles of the kingdom, the Sermon on the Mount is the constitution, and the commandments of Jesus are its laws or statutes.

First, the kingdom is established in the hearts of men. The principles of Jesus Christ are settled in our own spirit. We become citizens of the kingdom of heaven. The aggregate citizenship of the kingdom in this present age constitutes the real Church, which is His Body. And throughout the Church Age, the working of the Body is to be apparent in demonstrating to the world the practicability and desirability of the kingdom of heaven, that all men may desire the rule of Jesus, in the salvation of men.

It is the purpose of Jesus to make the Church, which is His Body, His entire representative in the world. Just as Jesus came to express God the Father to mankind, and Jesus was necessary to God in order that He might give an expression of Himself to the world, so the Church is necessary to Jesus Christ as an expression of Himself to the world.

Now the first principle that He laid down was this one: *"Blessed are the poor in spirit: for theirs is the kingdom of heaven"*

(Matthew 5:3). Usually we confuse this with the other one, *"Blessed are the meek"* (Matthew 5:5)—and we have commonly thought of one who is poor in spirit as being a meek, quiet person, possessing the spirit of meekness. But it is much more than that. The thing Jesus urged upon men was to practice what He had done Himself.

Jesus was the King of Glory, yet He laid down all His glory. He came to earth and took upon Himself our condition. *"He took not on him the nature of angels; but he took on him the seed of Abraham"* (Hebrews 2:16). He took upon Himself the condition of mankind, that is, of human nature's liability to sin. Therefore, He was *"in all points tempted like as we are, yet without sin"* (Hebrews 4:15). And because of the fact that He took upon Himself our nature and understood the temptations that are common to man, He is *"able to succour them that are tempted"* (Hebrews 2:18). He understands. He is a sympathetic Christ. Bless God!

Now see! *"Blessed are the poor in spirit"* (Matthew 5:3). Blessed is he who regards the interests of the kingdom of heaven as paramount to every other interest in the world, paramount to his own personal interest. Blessed is he whose interest in life, whose interest in the world, is used only to extend the interest of the kingdom of heaven. Blessed is he who has lost his own identity as an individual and has become a citizen of the kingdom. Blessed is he who sees the kingdom of heaven as the ultimate to be possessed. Blessed is he who forgets to hoard wealth for himself, but who uses all he has and all he is for the extension of the kingdom of heaven. It is putting the law of the love of God and of one another into practice.

So after Jesus had laid down the things that He possessed, then, bless God, He was able to say to us, as He had experienced it Himself, *"Blessed are the poor in spirit: for theirs is the kingdom of heaven"* (Matthew 5:3).

We commonly think as we read the Word of God that some of the teachings of Jesus were accidental, or were applied to a particular individual and to no one else. So we think of the rich young ruler who came to Jesus and said, *"Good Master, what shall I do to inherit eternal life?"* (Luke 18:18).

Jesus said, *"Thou knowest the commandments, Do not commit adultery, Do not kill, Do not steal, Do not bear false witness, Honour thy father and thy mother."*

The young man said: *"All these have I kept from my youth up."*

Then Jesus said to him, *"Yet lackest thou one thing: sell all that thou hast, and distribute unto the poor, and thou shalt have treasure in heaven: and come, follow me"* (Luke 18:20-22).

Don't you see, Jesus was applying that first principle of the kingdom to that young man. We have said that young man was covetous, and he loved his wealth, etc., and that was keeping him out of the kingdom of heaven. Not so. Jesus was applying one of the principles of the kingdom to that young man's life. He turned away sorrowful. He had not developed to the place where he could do that thing.

There is an apocryphal story that tells us that the rich young ruler was Barnabas. After the resurrection and the coming of the Holy Ghost, Barnabas received from heaven the thing Jesus had tried to impart to him. He forgot all about Barnabas, his own interest and his own desires, and he sold his great possessions and came with the others and laid them at the apostles' feet. *"Blessed are the poor in spirit: for theirs is the kingdom of heaven"* (Matthew 5:3). So Jesus was able, after all, to get the real thing in the heart of Barnabas that He desired in the beginning.

The real miracle of the Holy Ghost at Pentecost was not the outward demonstration of tongues, etc., but that it produced such intense unselfishness in the hearts of all baptized that they each sold their lands and estates and parted the money to every man as he had need. They were moved by God into one family. Their brother's interest was equal to their own. That was *"Blessed are the poor in spirit."*

The second principle of the kingdom is this: *"Blessed are they that mourn: for they shall be comforted"* (Matthew 5:4). This figure is taken from the old prophets who, when the nation sinned, took upon themselves the responsibility of the nation. They put sackcloth on their bodies, and ashes on their heads, and in mourning and tears went down before God for days and weeks until the people turned to God. They became the intercessors between God and man, and in some instances in the Word, we read where God looked and wondered. He wondered that there was no intercessor. There were no mourners who took upon themselves the responsibility of the sins of the people, who dared to stand between man and God.

We see how wonderfully Moses stood between God and the people. When God said to him, after they had made the golden calf, *"Let me alone...that I may consume them: and I will make of thee a great nation"* (Exodus 32:10), Moses said, "Not so, Lord. What will the Egyptians say; what will be the effect upon Thy great Name? Will they not say that their God destroyed them?" (See Exodus 32:11-12.) God had said to Moses, *"I will make of thee a great nation."* But Moses was big enough to turn aside the greatest honor that God could bestow upon a man—to become the father of a race. *"This people have sinned a great sin, and have made them gods of gold. Yet now, if thou wilt forgive their sin—; and if not, blot me, I pray thee, out of thy book"* (Exodus 32:31-32).

The prophet became the great intercessor. He took upon himself the burdens and sins of the people, and when he got down to confess, he did not say, "Oh, these people are so weak, and they do this and that."

But when he got down to pray he would say, "Lord God, WE are unworthy." He was ONE with his people. He was identified with them, as one with them. He was not putting any blame on them. He was big enough to take the whole blame, the entire responsibility, and go down before God and lay the whole matter before Him, until the blessed mercy of God was again given to the people.

"Blessed are the poor in spirit...Blessed are they that mourn." Blessed is the man who comprehends the purposes of God, who understands his responsibility and potential, who by God-given mourning and crying, turns the people to God. With heart yearning for sinners, he becomes a mourner

before God and takes the responsibility of fallen men on his own life. He goes down in tears and repentance before God, until men turn to God and the mercy of God is shown to mankind.

In the day that God puts the spirit of mourning upon Pentecost, it will be the gladdest day that heaven has ever known. Blessed be His precious Name!

It always jars me down in the depths of my spirit when I hear people say hard things about churches and sects. That is not our place. Our place is as intercessors...the ones who are to stand between the living and the dead, as those whom God can trust and use to pray down the power and mercy and blessing of God.

First we see that the kingdom is based on principles. Principles are greater than doctrines. Principles are the foundational stones upon which all other things rest. Doctrines are the rules, the details by which we endeavor to carry out things that the principles contain; but the principles are the great foundational stones upon which all things rest.

Absolute Consecration

Let us turn away from this until we see Jesus at the Jordan, consecrating Himself of His own life work; then we will understand how the Christian is to consecrate himself to carry out the principles.

The Word tells us that when Jesus began to be about 30 years of age, He came down to the River Jordan, where John was baptizing, and presented Himself for baptism. John looked in amazement on Him and said, *"I have need to be baptized of thee, and comest thou to me?"*

But Jesus said, *"Suffer it to be so now: for thus it becometh us to fulfil all righteousness"* (Matthew 3:14-15). Unto *"all righteousness."*

Listen! Hear the declaration to which Jesus Christ was baptized; it was His consecration unto *"all righteousness."* There was no further to go. It comprehends all there is of consecration and commitment unto the will of God, and all there is of good. Unto *"all righteousness."* Bless God!

So Jesus understandingly permitted Himself to be baptized of John unto *"all righteousness."* Now listen! You and I have also been baptized. But see! Immediately after He was baptized, something took place. First, the Spirit of God came upon Him as a dove and abode upon Him. Then we read He was led by the Spirit into the wilderness. It was the Holy Ghost Who led Him.

In Leviticus 16, we see one of the beautiful figures which will illustrate that to you. On the Day of Atonement there were brought two goats. The priest laid his hands upon the first goat and put a towrope around its neck; then the Levite took the towrope and led it three days into the barren sands of the wilderness, and left it there to die. That is the picture of the LIFE-DEATH of Jesus Christ.

The Holy Ghost is God's Levite. He put the towrope on the neck of Jesus Christ and led Him likewise three days—a year for a day, God's three days—into the wilderness. What for? To prove out, to test out, the real fact of His obedience unto God, and whether His consecration was going to stand. So the Spirit, the Holy Ghost, led Jesus into the wilderness.

Now I want you to see something. We are triune beings just as God Himself is triune. You will see the character of the consecration that Jesus made at the Jordan. God is TRIUNE. He is God the Father, God the Son and God the Holy Ghost. Man is also TRIUNE. The Word says, *"I pray God YOUR whole SPIRIT and SOUL and BODY be preserved blameless unto the coming of our Lord Jesus Christ"* (1 Thessalonians 5:23).

So Jesus, when He went into the wilderness, encountered a temptation peculiar to each separate department of His being. The Word of God says He fasted forty days and was an hungered. Satan came to Him and said, *"If thou be the Son of God, command that these stones be made bread"* (Matthew 4:3). But Jesus could not do it. If He had done that, He would have been exercising His own authority on His own behalf, and He had committed Himself unto *"all righteousness."* He only lived to express God; He only lived to express the Father. He said, "The words I speak, I speak not of Myself. The work that I do, I do not of Myself." (See John 14:10.)

All He said and all He did and all He was, was the expression of God the Father.

May the Lord give us an understanding of the absoluteness of what a real baptismal consecration ought to be. When an individual comes and commits himself to Christ once and for all, he ceases to be, he ceases to live on his own behalf, to live for himself any longer, but becomes the utter expression of Jesus Christ to mankind.

So Satan had no power to tempt a man who had made a consecration like that. The hunger calls of Jesus' body after He had fasted for forty days were not enough to turn Him aside from the consecration He had made to God.

The second temptation was one peculiar to the MIND (soul). He was taken to a pinnacle of the temple, and Satan said, "Do something spectacular; cast Yourself down; let the people see You are an unusual person and that You can do unusual things, and they will give You their acclaim."

Jesus could not do that. There was nothing, bless God, in the mind of Jesus

Christ that could tempt Him to be disobedient to the consecration He had made to God unto *"all righteousness."* So He turned the temptation aside.

The third temptation was one peculiar to the SPIRIT. By a supernatural power Jesus was permitted to see *"all the kingdoms of the world, and the glory of them,"* in a moment of time. Then Satan said unto Him, *"All these things will I give thee, if thou wilt fall down and worship me"* (Matthew 4:8-9). But Jesus turned him aside. No crossless crowning for the Son of God, no bloodless glory for my Lord. He had come to express God to the world. He had come to demonstrate one thing to you and me. That is, that man relying on God can have the victory over sin and Satan. Bless God! That is the peculiar thing about the life of Jesus Christ that makes Him dear to your heart and mine.

After going on the towrope of the Holy Ghost for three years as the first goat, through the sorrows and the trials and disappointments of life, ever ministering and blessing, though the world cursed Him, He was able to come as the second goat and present Himself as the sinless, spotless sacrifice unto God at the Cross.

If Jesus had fallen down anywhere along the line, if there had been a single instance where He had failed to express God to the world, He could never have been the Savior of the World. *"HE BECAME the author of eternal salvation..."* (Hebrews 5:9). He was honored of God in being permitted to die for mankind, having triumphed, having presented Himself the sinless, spotless sacrifice unto God. His blood flowed for all the race. Blessed be His Name!

Chapter 9

Preference or Conviction?
A Question of Destiny

Ray McCauley

> "'For I know the plans that I have for you,' declares the Lord, 'plans for welfare and not for calamity to give you a future and a hope.'"
> — JEREMIAH 29:11, NAS

I see them all too often. Christians who believe in healing...but stay sick. Who can quote scriptures about victory...yet live in defeat. Who want God's perfect will for their lives...but never seem to find it.

They know what the Word says. They believe it's true. Still, there's a striking difference between the lives of these Christians and the lives of early New Testament believers like Peter and John—a difference that continually trips them up and causes them to fall short of the full blessings of God.

Look at Acts 4 and you can see what I mean. There, we find Peter and John being cross-examined by the Jewish religious leaders who had arrested them for preaching and healing in the Name of Jesus. After hearing Peter's bold testimony, they conferred among themselves, saying:

> What shall we do to these men? for that indeed a notable miracle hath been done by them is manifest to all them that dwell in Jerusalem; and we cannot deny it. But that it spread no further among the people, let us straitly threaten them, that they speak henceforth to no man in this name. And they called them, and commanded them not to speak at all nor teach in the name of Jesus (verses 16-18).

Right there, we would have lost half our church congregations today. If they were told that the next time they returned to church they'd be arrested, they'd find somewhere else to go on Sunday.

> But Peter and John answered and said unto them, Whether it be

right in the sight of God to hearken unto you more than unto God, judge ye. For we cannot but speak the things which we have seen and heard (verses 19-20).

What's the difference between these two disciples and the Christians I described before? Preference and conviction. Many of today's Christians serve God out of preference. Preference is negotiable. It's a matter of choice. Peter and John served God out of conviction. And conviction is not negotiable. It's a requirement.

This is a major issue in the Body of Christ right now. I go to conventions and find that half the people who were there five years ago aren't there anymore. Why? Because they prefer to be somewhere else! They say, "We're not into studying the Word right now. We just want to dance and clap and fall down under the power of God. We just want to have fun."

Christians who live by preference instead of conviction are only "Word people" when it suits them. They'll hear some sermons preached on healing and they'll say, "That's

125

ONE WORD FROM GOD CAN CHANGE YOUR NATION

for me." Then, six months later, when the tire hits the tar, they back off.

They'll read in the Bible where Jesus said for us to go into all the world and preach the gospel to every creature. But then they'll say, "Well, Brother, I just felt like I needed to take some time off and not do anything for a while."

Far too many charismatic Christians right now live by what they feel instead of living by the Bible. When the Word tells them to do something they don't want to do, instead of fighting the fight of faith and overcoming the opposition of their flesh and the devil, they prefer to compromise.

High Price to Pay

If you want to know how much you can lose through that kind of compromise, just look through the Bible. Adam compromised God's law, followed his wife's sin and lost Paradise. Abraham compromised the trust, lied about Sarah and nearly lost his wife. Sarah compromised God's Word, put

Abraham and Hagar together, ended up with Ishmael and lost peace in the Middle East.

I could go on and on giving you scriptural examples of just how high the cost of compromise can be. But what's important for you to know is what such a lifestyle of compromise can cost you personally. And I can tell you. It will cost you your destiny.

Preference will not bring God's will to fulfillment in your life—only conviction will. That's why such a small percentage of the Body of Christ ever fulfills their divinely planned destiny.

They may do a great many "good things." But when this age is over and you stand before God, He is not going to judge you on what you've done. He's going to judge you on what He called you to do.

You see, just as God formed the prophetic ministry of Jeremiah before he was ever born (Jeremiah 1:5), God formed a plan and calling for every believer. But there are thousands of strong, Word-based believers whose lives are being shipwrecked because they think they have a choice about that calling. They get tired of the problems they face and say, "Who needs this?" Then they jump up and do something else. They may think that because they're not a preacher or an evangelist, it won't really matter, but that's not true.

You may be called to work in a certain office and be a witness for God there. If that's your calling and you fulfill it, you'll stand before God one day and receive a greater reward than some evangelist who was called to preach to 550 million people and only preached to 40 million.

It surprises most people when they hear that. They think certain people who have a higher profile and look more successful are greater in the kingdom of God. But God didn't say, "Well done thou good and successful servant." He said *"Well done, thou good and faithful servant"* (Matthew 25:21).

No Debate

Preference does not produce faithfulness. Only conviction will. As a pastor, I see demonstrations of that all the time. One guy came to me, for example, and said, "I've left the church because I had an argument with the parking lot attendant."

On the other hand, another guy came up to me and said, "The parking lot attendant was nasty to me, so the next week I walked up to him, grabbed him, kissed him on the cheek and said, 'Brother, God has placed me here. So I'm going to love you every Sunday until you love me.'"

What was the difference between those two people? One was a church member by preference, the other by conviction.

Conviction will keep you stable even when the pressure is on. I can tell you that from experience, because in South Africa we know about pressure. One friend of mine was called by God to build a 1,000-seat church building in a small town named Brits. The problem was, that town was the headquarters for a right-wing racist organization and this church was going to be integrated.

Immediately, this organization began attacking my friend's ministry. They got the town council to cut off his electricity and stop progress on the building. They even threatened his life.

He phoned me and said, "What must I do?"

"Well, I want to ask you something," I answered. "Did God put you there?"

"Yes," he said.

"Then there's no debate. That's the end of the discussion. They can threaten you. They can say they're going to beat you up. They can do whatever they like. But God placed you there, and the devil is not going to stop what God has divinely destined you to do."

Because that pastor was there out of conviction, he didn't cave in under pressure, and the building was completed in spite of the opposition. The night they dedicated that building, there were over 1,000 people in it—and more than 150 of them gave their lives to Christ!

Who Needs This?

If you want to fulfill God's will for your life, you're going to have to do it out of conviction, because preference won't carry you through the pressure. The greatest temptations you'll ever confront will be those the devil uses to pressure you to let go of your calling.

That's how it was in Jesus' life. In the Garden of Gethsemane, right before He was to complete God's plan for Him, He faced greater pressure than any of us will ever know. He could have become selfish. He could have turned around and said, "Do I need this? I haven't done anything to deserve this kind of treatment, and I'm not going to put up with it."

But He didn't. The Bible says He stripped Himself of His rightful privileges (Philippians 2:7, AMP) and said, *"Father...not My will, but (always) Yours, be done"* (Luke 22:42, AMP).

Imagine what would have happened if Jesus had just done what He personally preferred to do at that moment. A whole world would have been lost forever!

When we talk about fulfilling our callings, we're talking about destiny. We're talking about something that not only affects our own lives but the lives of countless others as well.

We can't afford to think just in terms of what we'd like to do right now; we must think in terms of eternity! That's what I have to do all the time, because God has called me to a dangerous place. A place that, naturally speaking, I'd often prefer not to be. A few years ago, for example, my country of South Africa was on the brink of civil war and God instructed me to initiate a peace accord. He said, *You know the two men who are leading this conflict, and you can stop it.*

I obeyed God and, over the next months, became involved in the drawing up of a peace document which culminated in the nation's leaders signing an historic National Peace Accord.

What would have happened if five years ago, my wife and I had left South Africa and moved to America just because we preferred it? We would have been in a mess and so would our country.

Some people say that every human being has his price. But people of conviction have no price. You can offer them an easy way out, offer them four times the salary they've been making, offer them anything to get them out of the will of God and they won't take it. They realize they've already been bought with the highest price of all—the precious blood of Jesus. They're committed.

Dare to be one of those committed believers. The next time the devil tries to pressure you to say, "Who needs this?" dare to say, "I do! I need to do everything God has called me to do. I need to live a life of conviction, not preference. And I can do it, because I can do all things through Christ Who strengthens me."

Dare to be uncompromising. You'll not only fulfill your divine destiny...in some ways, you'll change your country and the world.

Look Who's Crying Now

"And it shall come to pass in the last days, that the mountain of the Lord's house shall be established in the top of the mountains, and shall be exalted above the hills; and all nations shall flow unto it."
— ISAIAH 2:2

Gloria Copeland

People who don't say what they want don't get what they want.

That may sound like a simple statement, but I want you to think about it for a moment because, simple as it may seem, it is an important spiritual truth that many believers totally miss.

I don't know why that is. God emphasizes over and over throughout the Bible how important our words are. He tells us in Proverbs 18:21 that death and life are in the power of the tongue. He tells us in Mark 11:23 that *"whosoever shall say to*

*this mountain, Be thou removed, and be
thou cast into the sea; and shall not doubt
in his heart, but shall believe that those
things which he saith shall come to pass; he
shall have whatsoever he saith."*

He tells us in Romans 4:17 that to be
like Him we must speak things that *"be not
as though they were."* He tells us through
the Apostle Paul that *"I believed...therefore
have I spoken..."* (2 Corinthians 4:13).

There's no question about it—faith speaks!

Notice I didn't say faith whines and
cries. You'd think it did by the way many
Christians talk. "Oh my," they'll say. "Things
are so bad. I just don't know what I'm going
to do. I lost my job. My arthritis is acting
up and my kids are a mess. I sure hope God
does something to help us quick!"

But that's not how faith talks. Faith
boldly proclaims the Word of God.

Faith isn't a bit wimpy. Faith doesn't
whine around, wondering if things are going
to turn out. Faith speaks as Jesus did in
Mark 4 when He was in a ship, crossing the
sea with His disciples:

And there arose a great storm of wind, and the waves beat into the ship, so that it was now full. And he was in the hinder part of the ship, asleep on a pillow: and they awake him, and say unto him, Master, carest thou not that we perish? And he arose, and rebuked the wind, and said unto the sea, Peace, be still. And the wind ceased, and there was a great calm. And he said unto them, Why are ye so fearful? how is it that ye have no faith? (verses 37-40).

Notice when Jesus' disciples came to Him in a panic, He didn't start crying, "Father, see this storm? We're about to drown here! If You don't do something, we're all going to die!" Do you know what would have happened if He'd have done that?

Nothing would have changed.

The storm would have raged on. The ship would have sunk, and Jesus' ministry would have sunk right along with it.

You see, Jesus had to operate by faith just as we do. He was in a natural body, and He operated as a man in the earth. Everything He did, He did by faith. So when He confronted a situation that was contrary to the will of God, He spoke to it. He spoke to the wind and sea and said, *"Peace, be still."*

He didn't talk about the problem—He spoke the end result. He said not what already was, but what He wanted to come to pass.

Why Didn't You Say Something?

You may be thinking, "Well, I know all about the power of words. I know I'm supposed to say what I want to come to pass."

That may be true. But knowing it and doing it are two different things.

The Lord impressed that fact to me very strongly one day. He reminded me of what happens when a married couple goes out to eat. (You'll recognize this scenario. I think we've all done it. I know Ken and I certainly have.)

"Where do you want to go eat, honey?" the husband will ask.

"Oh, I don't care. Wherever you want to go is fine with me," she'll answer.

Taking his wife at her word, the husband will go to his favorite restaurant. The problem is, the wife doesn't really like that one. Once they get there and start to order, she'll be acting a little aggravated.

"What's wrong?"

"Oh, nothing," snaps the wife.

"Something is bothering you. What is it?"

"I didn't want to eat here. I wanted to eat somewhere else."

"Well, why didn't you say something?" he'll ask in exasperation.

Now that's just a small example, but it illustrates a very solemn truth. Someday when our earthly lives are finished, when we stand before Jesus, someone might say, "Lord, I really needed clothes for my children when I was on earth...I really needed healing for my body...I really needed deliverance from my circumstances."

And I can just hear Jesus saying to us just what the husband said to his wife, "Well, why didn't you say something?!"

Those words would shock many Christians. They think they're sitting around in the midst of their crises waiting for God to act—when all the time, He's waiting for them. Jesus is waiting for each one of us to take the power and dominion He gave to us and use it to put those devil-generated crises where they belong—under our feet! He's waiting on us to take authority in our personal lives, in our families, in our cities and in our nations.

Jesus said, *"All authority in heaven and on earth has been given to me. Therefore [you] go...!"* (Matthew 28:18-19, NIV). You lay hands on the sick and they'll recover. You cast out the devil. You pray for your nation. In other words, Jesus was saying, "I'm giving you My authority, so use it!"

God has given you authority over the things in your life just as He gave Adam authority in the Garden of Eden. You have authority over your family and your household. But if you don't exercise your authority, the devil will come in and take over your garden just as he took over Adam's garden.

When Ken and I first got born again, we didn't understand that. As a result, we just kept bumping around in the same old ruts we'd been in before we were saved. We stayed just as broke and sick as everybody else in the world.

Oh, we knew God worked miracles. Ken saw them firsthand when he was working as a co-pilot, flying Oral Roberts to his healing meetings. When they would arrive at the meeting, it was Ken's job to get the people in the invalid tent ready before Brother Roberts came in to minister to them.

The invalid tent was the place where the people went who were too sick to go into the regular meeting. Most of them were on stretchers or in the last stages of some terminal disease.

Yet as Brother Roberts laid his hands on those people, Ken saw amazing miracles. One woman with cancer spit that cancer up, right in the middle of the floor. A girl, who came in strapped to a board because she was totally paralyzed, jumped straight up when Brother Roberts touched her and began to run around the tent totally healed.

Ken saw those miracles with his own eyes. But do you know what? They didn't do anything for our family. It was when we heard that Jesus had already borne *our* sicknesses and carried *our* diseases that our personal lives changed.

It was when we saw in the Word of God that we had authority over sickness and began to say so, that we began to get free. When we realized that we weren't the sick trying to get healed, but that we were the healed and the devil was trying to steal our health, we began to take dominion and say, "Devil, get out of here!" And he would flee and take his sickness with him.

Of course, it's a thrill to see God work miracles. But you can't live day in, day out on miracles. What will change your life is taking hold of the authority that belongs to you in the Word of God. If you'll do that, you can keep the devil under your feet where he belongs.

Get Out of My Garden

I'm not saying the devil will stop coming to your house trying to kill, steal and destroy. He'll never stop trying to do those things until God puts him away. What I'm saying is that he won't be able to succeed, because you won't be going to God and crying, "Please do something about the devil, Lord. He's making my child sick."

You'll do it yourself. You'll take the Name of Jesus and the devil-casting-out power He gave you and say, "Satan, in the Name of Jesus, get your hands off my baby. He is healed by Jesus' stripes!" Then keep saying what you want to come to pass—the end result.

You see, Satan is an outlaw. God has given us laws to keep him in line, but he won't abide by them unless we enforce those laws.

That's not really surprising. Things work the same way in the natural realm. In the United States, for example, we have laws against selling drugs. We have laws against murder. We have laws against stealing. But if those laws aren't enforced, what happens? Thieves and murderers continue to operate. The laws have to be enforced.

Once you understand that, you'll see why Satan works so hard to get you to talk about your problems instead of God's promises. He knows your authority to enforce God's law is in your words. If he can get your words going in his direction, he can get authority over your life—even though it doesn't belong to him.

Satan doesn't care what belongs to him. He's a thief. He's a killer. He takes what he can get. So you have to use the Word of God on him when he tries to come into your garden and spoil it.

That's what Adam should have done when Satan showed up in his garden. The first time that creature opened his mouth to question the Word of God, Adam should have said, "Get out of my garden, you serpent!"

And that's what you and I should do too. The first time the devil starts trying to bring doubt and unbelief to us—*Do you really think God is going to heal you? Do you really think God is going to send you the money to pay that bill?*—we should just tell him to take his lies and get out of our lives!

How do you do that? Just say, "You doubt, you unbelief, you fear—in the Name of Jesus, leave my presence. Yes, I really do believe the Word of God!" Then start quoting that Word and don't stop.

Just keep on speaking and studying what the Word of God says about your situation until it's that Word you're hearing in your heart all day instead of those lies of the devil.

Jesus said, *"If ye abide in me, and my words abide in you, ye shall ask what ye will, and it shall be done unto you"* (John 15:7). *The Amplified Bible* says, *"If you live in Me...and My words remain in you and continue to live in your hearts...."*

It's the Word that's talking to you that's alive in you.

If God's Word isn't talking in your heart, it's not alive in there. So you need to bring it to life by putting it in your heart and mind day and night. Keep it fresh on your mind every day—and when Satan comes to seduce you, it will rise up and speak against him.

Don't Buy the Lie

Remember this: Satan can't force you to do anything. He doesn't have the power. All he can do is make a presentation and try to sell you the lies he is peddling. He can't make you buy them. He can only present them. You have a choice whether to take him up on his sorry deal or rebuke him and command him to leave you.

So when he makes you a presentation, learn not to toy with it. Don't take the bait. Instead, learn to immediately turn away from his doubts and start thinking and speaking the Word of God instead. Ask yourself: *What does the Word say that guarantees me the very thing the devil just tried to make me doubt?*

Get in the Word of God and find out the real truth. That's where your authority is—in the truth. Satan will lie to you, cheat you, trick you, deceive you and bait you into bondage if you'll let him. But God will always tell you the truth. And that truth will make you free.

Once you really know the truth of your authority in Christ Jesus, you won't sit around imprisoned by mountains of sickness, poverty and defeat. You won't spend your days crying about how bad things are. You'll spend your days telling those mountains to be cast into the sea.

Instead of acting like a whiner, you'll be more than a conqueror in Christ. You'll kick the devil out of your garden with the words of your mouth. And as you stand in triumph with your needs met, your body healed and your heart rejoicing, you can laugh right in the face of that old snake as he slinks away complaining about his defeat.

The Bridge Between Two Worlds

"For unto us a child is born, unto us a son is given: and the government shall be upon his shoulder: and his name shall be called Wonderful, Counsellor, The mighty God, The everlasting Father, The Prince of Peace."
— ISAIAH 9:6

Kenneth Copeland

Everyone knows what a great place heaven is. It has everything—wealth so immense that streets are made of gold, health so abundant that sickness can't exist there, joy so plentiful it forever extinguishes all sorrow.

Christians everywhere dream of going there when they die.

But just imagine for a moment how wonderful it would be if you could have access to the riches of heaven right now. Think what it would be like if God would build a bridge between the realm of heaven and earth so that those boundless heavenly supplies could flow down to meet the needs in your life today.

It's a wonderful thought, isn't it?

But do you know what's even more wonderful? The bridge has been built.

Most people can't even believe such a thing is possible! That's because, in their minds, the world of the spirit, where heaven exists, isn't quite real. They think of it as a hazy, spooky place where people float around like "Casper the Friendly Ghost." So they can't understand how the "reality" of this physical world of matter and the "unreality" of the spiritual world ever could be connected.

I used to think that way too. But some years ago, when God began to teach me about these things, He set me straight and renewed my mind. He told me that the spectrum of reality includes both the spiritual world and the material world. He also informed me that, contrary to popular belief, the spiritual world is not only just as real as this physical world, but it is more real!

Just as material things are tangible to us here on earth, spiritual things are tangible in the world of the spirit. People don't float through walls in heaven. Spiritual things are firm there, just like here. For example, in heaven a table is a table. You can set things on it. Your fork doesn't fall through it when you sit down to eat.

You see, back before God created the earth, the spiritual world was the only one that existed. In fact, it was the pattern on which material world was based.

God didn't create earth first and then heaven. He created heaven first and then earth. Earth was a carbon copy of heaven—and it was not created to stand alone. God created this material world to be joined to its mother world—the world of the spirit—because that world held all the answers and supplies this earth would ever need. He created them to be united by a supernatural bridge.

In short, God intended there to be heaven on earth. And there was...until the bridge was broken.

And God Said

What was this bridge? What was the divine link that connected these two worlds? Look at the book of Genesis, and you can see it for yourself. There the Bible tells us: *"In the beginning God created the heaven and the earth. And the earth was without form, and void; and darkness was upon the face of the deep. And the spirit of God moved upon the face of the waters"* (Genesis 1:1-2).

Notice in these first two verses that the Holy Spirit was already moving on the face of the water, yet nothing was happening. He was just moving. But then, *"God said, Let there be light; and there was light"* (verse 3).

God said it—and the Holy Spirit did it!

And God said, Let there be a firmament in the midst of the waters... and it was so....And God said, Let the waters under the heaven be gathered together unto one place, and let the dry land appear: and it was so....And God said, Let the earth bring forth grass...and it was so....And God said, Let there be

lights in the firmament of the heaven...and it was so....And God said, Let the waters bring forth abundantly the moving creature... and God saw that it was good.... And God said, Let the earth bring forth the living creature...and it was so....And God said, Let us make man in our image...and it was so (verses 6-30).

An English teacher might consider Genesis 1 to be too repetitive. After all, the same ideas could have been expressed by simply saying, "God said, 'Let there be light; let there be a firmament; let the waters be gathered; let the earth bring forth'...and it was so."

It seems as though God wasted words by repeating Himself. But God doesn't waste words. He engineered the writing of Genesis so it would read exactly as He wanted. He risked being extremely redundant by saying eight times in this first chapter, *"God said...and it was so."*

The reason? He was trying to communicate something very important to us. He was revealing to us how He brings things from the world of the spirit into the world of matter. He was showing us the bridge.

"A bridge?" you ask. "Why would God need a bridge? He was creating the earth, He wasn't moving it from one place to another."

Yes, He was. You see, in a sense, this material world existed even before its creation. It existed within the Spirit of God.

That may sound complicated, but it's really not. If you think of it in natural terms, you can see it clearly. For example, where was the Model-T Ford before Henry Ford built it? Inside Henry Ford! He created it. If it didn't exist within him, he never could have built it.

In that same way, this material world was once in God's innermost being. How did He bring it forth? By His Word.

Let Us Make Man

God said...and it was so. God repeated that phrase again and again in Genesis 1 so we would clearly know that His Word was the way He created man himself, and not just grass and trees and animals. God specifically wanted us to understand that the race of man was first brought into being by His Word.

Sadly enough, many people miss that point altogether because they mix up Genesis' account of the formation of man's body with the creation of mankind. Man's body was formed from the dust of the ground. (Of course, the dust itself was there because *"God said..."*; thus even our bodies exist by virtue of God's Word.) But that body was a lifeless thing until God *"breathed into his nostrils the breath of life; and man became a living soul"* (Genesis 2:7).

The concept of God breathing into us the breath (the Hebrew word is actually spirit) of life would be very mysterious to us if we didn't have Genesis 1. But, praise God, we do—and it tells us exactly how it happened.

"God said, Let us make man in our image..." (Genesis 1:26).

Man became when God said.

Because of the English translation of that verse, some folks have the impression

155

that God was just speaking casually there. They think God looked around that day and said, "Hey, I have an idea. Let's make a man! Don't you think that would be nice?"

If you were to read the Hebrew text, however, you'd realize God was giving a forceful command. He literally said, "Man, be after Our image!"

Those words went into that body and brought spiritual life. God's words became Adam.

God's words didn't stop being life once mankind was created. Proverbs 4 tells us that His words are still *"life unto those that find them, and health to all their flesh"* (verse 22). Jesus confirmed it by saying, *"The words that I speak unto you, they are spirit, and they are life"* (John 6:63).

As long as God's Word was alive in Adam, he was as much a part of the world of the spirit as he was part of the material world. He and God were connected together. They walked and talked together daily.

Then the bridge was broken.

THE BRIDGE BETWEEN TWO WORLDS

Everyone who's ever been to church knows how it happened. Man and woman bowed their knee to the devil in the Garden of Eden, and sin entered the material world and death by sin. When it did, the material world was separated from its mother world.

The life inside mankind died. Their bodies lived on, but the Word that had connected them to God and to the heavenly realm had been snuffed out.

With the supply lines to heaven cut off, pain, poverty, disease and death ran rampant on the earth—needs went unmet, problems unsolved, questions unanswered. And so it continued for 4,000 years.

The Word Was Made Flesh

Then one night, over the little city of Bethlehem, an angel exploded with joy, announcing the good news: "Peace on earth. Good will toward men!"

Jesus had been born into the earth. The Word—that same Word that had brought life to Adam—was back, and as far as God was concerned, the war with man was over. Heaven and earth were connected again.

John 1 says it this way:

> In the beginning was the Word, and the Word was with God, and the Word was God. The same was in the beginning with God. All things were made by him [the Word]; and without him was not any thing made that was made. In him was life; and the life was the light of men.... He came unto his own, and his own received him not. But as many as received him, to them gave he power to become the sons of God, even to them that believe on his name: Which were born, not of blood, nor of the will of the flesh, nor of the will of man, but of God. And the Word was made flesh, and dwelt among us... (verses 1-4, 11-14).

Do you realize what that means? It means that you, as a born-again believer, are once again hooked up to the world of the spirit. The Word is alive inside you.

Like Adam before the Fall, you're as much a part of heaven as you are a part of earth.

You've been reborn, *"not of corruptible seed, but of incorruptible, by the word of God, which liveth and abideth for ever"* (1 Peter 1:23). Because the Word lives, you live. You're created by it!

You and I are a part of the largest race of people that has ever lived on the face of the earth, and it is not determined by the color of our skin or what nation we're from. It is determined by the blood of Jesus! We are a new people. We are a supernatural, reborn race! We are people of the spirit world—like God.

That's why Jesus went to the cross. He endured the shame of it so He could re-establish the bridge between heaven and earth...not just through one Man but through millions like you and me.

Act Like It!

When you get a revelation of that fact, you won't be dragging around trying to make do with the pathetic resources of this devil-dominated world system. You'll realize you have the power of heaven available to you—the same power that created this planet in the first place.

It's true! Right now the Spirit of God is moving on the face of the earth just as He was in the book of Genesis. He filled this atmosphere nearly 2,000 years ago on the Day of Pentecost. He came rushing in with the sound of a mighty wind (Acts 2:2), and He is still here—upon us, in us and among us.

But now, just as in the beginning, He is waiting for the Word of God.

Who is going to speak that Word?

You are! The power of life and death has been put into the tongue of the believer! The heavenly connection has been put inside you!

It is an awesome thought. God chose us before the foundation of the world to carry out the ministry of reconciliation, by His Word bringing the power and supply of heaven to a starving world (2 Corinthians 5:18-20). It was this astounding message that the Apostle Paul preached everywhere he went in order...

> To make all men see what is the fellowship [their part] of the mystery, which from the beginning of the world hath been hid in God, who created all things by Jesus [His anointed]: To the intent that now unto the principalities and powers in heavenly places might be known by the church the manifold wisdom of God, According to the eternal purpose which he purposed in [The Anointed] Jesus our Lord (Ephesians 3:9-11).

What was Paul saying in those verses? Just this: That God's intention, the revelation that was inside Him when He created the worlds, was that His wisdom might be made known to all created spirits, all angels (including the devil and his crowd) and all of heaven...through the believer.

You and I are living demonstrations of the wisdom and power of God Himself. Angels can't understand us. They look in awe, wondering how the likes of you and me, who were such sinful, pitiful creatures, could be re-created in the very likeness of God.

They stand amazed that we have been chosen not only to be reborn by the Word, but to be entrusted with it, and to rule and reign by the power of that Word with Jesus Himself.

Satan hates us because we've been given that right. He is eaten up with jealousy because he wanted it for himself. In fact, when Satan realized that God created by the words He spoke, he tried to gain that power by saying, *"I will be like the most High"* (Isaiah 14:14). But the moment he did, he was doomed because as an angel, he had no God-given right to say such words.

Yet you looked in the Word and said, "I'll be like Jesus," and instead of being destroyed, you were born again! You were re-created in His image just as you said.

And that was just the beginning. From that time on, all God's Words became yours for the taking. When sickness attacked you, you could take the Word *"by whose stripes ye were healed"* (1 Peter 2:24), put it in your heart, speak it out your mouth and be healed. When you were fed up with poverty and lack, you could pick up your Bible and run the devil out of your household with words like "All my needs are met according to God's riches in glory by Christ Jesus." (See Philippians 4:19.)

Then you could tap into the wealth of heaven because you're linked up with Jesus, the King of kings and Lord of lords. And through Him you have access to all the power and might of God Himself.

Listen, according to the Bible, we are the most astoundingly powerful creatures God has ever made. It's time we started to act like it!

It's time we stopped sitting around crying, waiting for God to change our world and meet our needs. He has already done everything He is going to do about those things. He sent Jesus to whip the devil and take back this earth.

Jesus did it too, and after He did, He turned to us and said, *"All power is given*

163

unto me in heaven and in earth. Go ye therefore..." (Matthew 28:18-19).

In other words, "I have given you My Word...now go use it!"

I believe it's time we started to obey Him by getting God's Word into our hearts and then speaking it out our mouths in faith.

After all, that Word has the same power now that it had when God said, *"Let there be light!"* It has the power to change not only our own lives, but also our families, our cities, our nations, our world.

For those who dare to believe and to speak, it still has the power to bridge two worlds...and produce days of heaven on earth.

A Prayer for Our Nations

"And he taught, saying unto them, Is it not written, My house shall be called of all nations the house of prayer?"
— MARK 11:17

Daily, international events are setting the stage for Jesus' return. As believers in every land continue to pray on behalf of their leaders, God is pouring out His Spirit, making tremendous power available to guide the governments of every nation according to His divine will and plan. As you stand for your nation, you can pray the following:

O, God in heaven, I come before You in the Name of Jesus on behalf of the leaders of this nation. You said the heart of the king is in Your hand and You will turn it whichever way You choose (Proverbs 21:1). I ask You to direct the heart and mind of (the name of your nation's leader) to make decisions that will lead our country in Your ways and according to Your Word.

I thank You, Lord, for bringing change to the politics of our nation. Thank You for changing the voices of influence to speak in agreement with Your Word. I ask You to send laborers filled with the spirit of wisdom and might to surround our leaders with godly counsel and insight. I also ask You to remove from positions of authority those who stubbornly oppose righteousness, and replace them with men and women who will follow You and Your appointed course for (the name of your nation).

As we enter the final hours of the last days, I ask for the spirit of faith, the workings of miracles, for signs, wonders, gifts and demonstrations of the Holy Spirit and power to be in strong operation. Let believers in (the name of your nation) and in every land be unified to stand strong by faith in Jesus, the Anointed One and His Anointing, that Your glory may be revealed in all the earth.

Thank You, Lord, that these requests come to pass. I believe I receive. Amen.

Scriptures for Further Prayer and Meditation

2 Chronicles 7:14

"If my people, which are called by my name, shall humble themselves, and pray, and seek my face, and turn from their wicked ways; then will I hear from heaven, and will forgive their sin, and will heal their land."

Psalm 22:27

"All the ends of the world shall remember and turn unto the Lord: and all the kindreds of the nations shall worship before thee."

Psalm 22:28

"For the kingdom is the Lord's: and he is the governor among the nations."

Psalm 57:9

"I will praise thee, O Lord, among the people: I will sing unto thee among the nations."

Psalm 67:4

"O let the nations be glad and sing for joy: for thou shalt judge the people righteously, and govern the nations upon earth. Selah."

Psalm 72:11

"Yea, all kings shall fall down before him: all nations shall serve him."

Psalm 72:17

"His name shall endure for ever: his name shall be continued as long as the sun: and men shall be blessed in him: all nations shall call him blessed."

Psalm 82:8

"Arise, O God, judge the earth: for thou shalt inherit all nations."

Psalm 113:4

"The Lord is high above all nations, and his glory above the heavens."

Psalm 117:1-2

"O praise the Lord, all ye nations: praise him, all ye people. For his merciful kindness

is great toward us: and the truth of the Lord endureth for ever. Praise ye the Lord."

Proverbs 14:34

"Righteousness exalteth a nation: but sin is a reproach to any people."

Proverbs 21:1

"The king's heart is in the hand of the Lord, as the rivers of water: he turneth it whithersoever he will."

Proverbs 29:2

"When the righteous are in authority, the people rejoice: but when the wicked beareth rule, the people mourn."

Isaiah 2:2

"And it shall come to pass in the last days, that the mountain of the Lord's house shall be established in the top of the mountains, and shall be exalted above the hills; and all nations shall flow unto it."

Isaiah 5:26

"And he will lift up an ensign to the nations from far, and will hiss unto them

from the end of the earth: and, behold, they shall come with speed swiftly."

Isaiah 9:6

"For unto us a child is born, unto us a son is given: and the government shall be upon his shoulder: and his name shall be called Wonderful, Counsellor, The mighty God, The everlasting Father, The Prince of Peace."

Isaiah 60:1-3

"Arise, shine; for thy light is come, and the glory of the Lord is risen upon thee. For, behold, the darkness shall cover the earth, and gross darkness the people: but the Lord shall arise upon thee, and his glory shall be seen upon thee. And the Gentiles shall come to thy light, and kings to the brightness of thy rising."

Malachi 3:12

"And all nations shall call you blessed: for ye shall be a delightsome land, saith the Lord of hosts."

Matthew 16:19

"And I will give unto thee the keys of the kingdom of heaven: and whatsoever

thou shalt bind on earth shall be bound in heaven: and whatsoever thou shalt loose on earth shall be loosed in heaven."

Matthew 18:19-20

"Again I say unto you, That if two of you shall agree on earth as touching any thing that they shall ask, it shall be done for them of my Father which is in heaven. For where two or three are gathered together in my name, there am I in the midst of them."

Matthew 24:6-7

"And ye shall hear of wars and rumours of wars: see that ye be not troubled: for all these things must come to pass, but the end is not yet. For nation shall rise against nation, and kingdom against kingdom: and there shall be famines, and pestilences, and earthquakes, in divers places."

Matthew 24:14

"And this gospel of the kingdom shall be preached in all the world for a witness unto all nations; and then shall the end come."

Matthew 28:19-20

"Go ye therefore, and teach all nations, baptizing them in the name of the Father, and of the Son, and of the Holy Ghost: Teaching them to observe all things whatsoever I have commanded you: and, lo, I am with you always, even unto the end of the world. Amen."

Mark 11:17

"And he taught, saying unto them, Is it not written, My house shall be called of all nations the house of prayer? but ye have made it a den of thieves."

Mark 13:10-11

"And the gospel must first be published among all nations. But when they shall lead you, and deliver you up, take no thought beforehand what ye shall speak, neither do ye premeditate: but whatsoever shall be given you in that hour, that speak ye: for it is not ye that speak, but the Holy Ghost."

Romans 13:1, NKJV

"Let every soul be subject to the governing authorities. For there is no authority except from God, and the authorities that exist are appointed by God."

Galatians 3:8-9

"And the scripture, foreseeing that God would justify the heathen through faith, preached before the gospel unto Abraham, saying, In thee shall all nations be blessed. So then they which be of faith are blessed with faithful Abraham."

Galatians 3:27-29

"For as many of you as have been baptized into Christ have put on Christ. There is neither Jew nor Greek, there is neither bond nor free, there is neither male nor female: for ye are all one in Christ Jesus. And if ye be Christ's, then are ye Abraham's seed, and heirs according to the promise."

Ephesians 2:11-13

"Wherefore remember, that ye being in time past Gentiles in the flesh, who are

called Uncircumcision by that which is called the Circumcision in the flesh made by hands; That at that time ye were without Christ, being aliens from the commonwealth of Israel, and strangers from the covenants of promise, having no hope, and without God in the world: But now in Christ Jesus ye who sometimes were far off are made nigh by the blood of Christ."

Ephesians 2:18-19

"For through him we both have access by one Spirit unto the Father. Now therefore ye are no more strangers and foreigners, but fellowcitizens with the saints, and of the household of God."

Ephesians 6:10-12

"Finally, my brethren, be strong in the Lord, and in the power of his might. Put on the whole armour of God, that ye may be able to stand against the wiles of the devil. For we wrestle not against flesh and blood, but against principalities, against powers, against the rulers of the darkness of this world, against spiritual wickedness in high places."

Philippians 2:9-11

"Wherefore God also hath highly exalted him, and given him a name which is above every name: That at the name of Jesus every knee should bow, of things in heaven, and things in earth, and things under the earth; And that every tongue should confess that Jesus Christ is Lord, to the glory of God the Father."

1 Timothy 2:1-2

"I exhort therefore, that, first of all, supplications, prayers, intercessions, and giving of thanks, be made for all men; For kings, and for all that are in authority; that we may lead a quiet and peaceable life in all godliness and honesty."

1 John 5:4

"For whatsoever is born of God overcometh the world: and this is the victory that overcometh the world, even our faith."

Revelation 15:4

"Who shall not fear thee, O Lord, and glorify thy name? for thou only art holy: for

all nations shall come and worship before thee; for thy judgments are made manifest."

Prayer for Salvation and Baptism in the Holy Spirit

Heavenly Father, I come to You in the Name of Jesus. Your Word says, *"Who-soever shall call on the name of the Lord shall be saved"* (Acts 2:21). I am calling on You. I pray and ask Jesus to come into my heart and be Lord over my life according to Romans 10:9-10. *"If thou shalt confess with thy mouth the Lord Jesus, and shalt believe in thine heart that God hath raised him from the dead, thou shalt be saved. For with the heart man believeth unto righteousness; and with the mouth confession is made unto salvation."* I do that now. I confess that Jesus is Lord, and I believe in my heart that God raised Him from the dead.

I am now reborn! I am a Christian—a child of Almighty God! I am saved! You also said in Your Word, *"If ye then, being evil, know how to give good gifts unto your children: HOW MUCH MORE shall your heavenly Father give the Holy Spirit to them that ask him?"* (Luke 11:13). I'm also asking You to fill me with the Holy Spirit. Holy Spirit, rise up within me as I praise God. I fully expect to speak with other tongues as You give me the utterance (Acts 2:4).

Begin to praise God for filling you with the Holy Spirit. Speak those words and syllables you receive—not in your own language, but the language given to you by the Holy Spirit. You have to use your own voice. God will not force you to speak. Worship and praise Him in your heavenly language—in other tongues.

Continue with the blessing God has given you and pray in tongues each day.

You are a born-again, Spirit-filled believer. You'll never be the same!

Find a good Word of God preaching church, and become a part of a church family who will love and care for you as you love and care for them.

We need to be hooked up to each other. It increases our strength in God. It's God's plan for us.

Books Available
From
Kenneth Copeland Ministries

by Kenneth Copeland
* A Ceremony of Marriage
  A Matter of Choice
  Covenant of Blood
  Faith and Patience—The Power Twins
* Freedom From Fear
  Giving and Receiving
  Honor—Walking in Honesty, Truth and Integrity
  How to Conquer Strife
  How to Discipline Your Flesh
  How to Receive Communion
  Living at the End of Time—
      A Time of Supernatural Increase
  Love Never Fails
  Managing God's Mutual Funds
* Now Are We in Christ Jesus
* Our Covenant With God
* Prayer—Your Foundation for Success
* Prosperity: The Choice Is Yours
  Rumors of War
* Sensitivity of Heart
* Six Steps to Excellence in Ministry
  Sorrow Not! Winning Over Grief and Sorrow
* The Decision Is Yours
* The Force of Faith
* The Force of Righteousness
  The Image of God in You
  The Laws of Prosperity
* The Mercy of God
  The Miraculous Realm of God's Love
  The Outpouring of the Spirit—The Result of Prayer
* The Power of the Tongue
  The Power to Be Forever Free
  The Troublemaker
* The Winning Attitude

Turn Your Hurts Into Harvests
* Welcome to the Family
* You Are Healed!
Your Right-Standing With God

by Gloria Copeland
* And Jesus Healed Them All
Are You Ready?
Build Your Financial Foundation
Build Yourself an Ark
Fight On!
God's Prescription for Divine Health
God's Success Formula
God's Will for You
God's Will for Your Healing
God's Will Is Prosperity
* God's Will Is the Holy Spirit
* Harvest of Health
Hidden Treasures
Living Contact
Living in Heaven's Blessings Now
* Love—The Secret to Your Success
No Deposit—No Return
Pleasing the Father
Pressing In—It's Worth It All
Shine On!
The Power to Live a New Life
The Unbeatable Spirit of Faith
This Same Jesus
* Walk in the Spirit
Walk With God
Well Worth the Wait

Books Co-Authored by Kenneth and Gloria Copeland
Family Promises
Healing Promises
Prosperity Promises

* From Faith to Faith—A Daily Guide to Victory
From Faith to Faith—A Perpetual Calendar

One Word From God Series
- One Word From God Can Change Your Destiny
- One Word From God Can Change Your Family
- One Word From God Can Change Your Finances
- One Word From God Can Change Your Health

Over the Edge—A Youth Devotional
Over the Edge Xtreme Planner for Students—
    Designed for the School Year

Pursuit of His Presence—A Daily Devotional
Pursuit of His Presence—A Perpetual Calendar

Other Books Published by KCP
The First 30 Years—A Journey of Faith
    The story of the lives of
        Kenneth and Gloria Copeland.
Real People. Real Needs. Real Victories.
    A book of testimonies to encourage your faith.

John G. Lake—His Life, His Sermons,
    His Boldness of Faith
The Holiest of All by Andrew Murray
The New Testament in Modern Speech by
    Richard Francis Weymouth

Products Designed for Today's Children and Youth
Baby Praise Board Book
Noah's Ark Coloring Book
The *Shout!* Super-Activity Book

Commander Kellie and the Superkid Adventure Novels
#1 The Mysterious Presence
#2 The Quest for the Second Half
#3 Escape From Jungle Island
#4 In Pursuit of the Enemy

SWORD Adventure Book

* Available in Spanish

WE'RE HERE FOR YOU!

Join Kenneth and Gloria Copeland and the *Believer's Voice of Victory* broadcast Monday through Friday and every Sunday. Learn how faith in God's Word can take your life from ordinary to extraordinary.

It's some of the most in-depth teaching you'll ever hear on subjects like faith and healing, deliverance and prosperity, protection and hope. And it's all designed to get you where you want to be—*on top!* The teachings are by some of today's best-known ministers, including Kenneth and Gloria Copeland, Jerry Savelle, Charles Capps, Creflo A. Dollar Jr., Kellie Copeland and Edwin Louis Cole.

Whether it's before breakfast, during lunch or after a long day at the office, plan to make *Believer's Voice of Victory* a daily part of your prayer life. See for yourself how one word from God can change your life forever.

You can catch the *Believer's Voice of Victory* broadcast on the following cable and satellite channels:

Sunday
9-9:30 p.m. ET
Cable*/G5,
Channel 3—TBN

Monday through Friday
7-7:30 p.m. ET
Cable*/G1,
Channel 17—INSP

Monday through Friday
6-6:30 a.m. ET
Cable*/G5,
Channel 7—WGN

Monday through Friday
11-11:30 a.m. ET
Cable*/G5,
Channel 3—TBN

Monday through Friday
6:30-7 a.m. ET
Cable*/G5,
Channel 20—BET

Monday through Friday
10:30-11 a.m. CT
Cable*/Spacenet 3,
Transponder 13 - KMPX

*Check your local listings for more times and stations in your area.

WE'RE HERE FOR YOU!

Believer's Voice of Victory Television Broadcast

Join Kenneth and Gloria Copeland and the *Believer's Voice of Victory* broadcasts Monday through Friday and on Sunday each week, and learn how faith in God's Word can take your life from ordinary to extraordinary. This is some of the best teaching you'll ever hear, designed to get you where you want to be— *on top!*

You can catch the *Believer's Voice of Victory* broadcast on your local, cable or satellite channels.

* Check your local listings for
times and stations in your area.

Believer's Voice of Victory Magazine

Enjoy inspired teaching and encouragement from Kenneth and Gloria Copeland each month in the *Believer's Voice of Victory* magazine. Also included are real-life testimonies of God's miraculous power and divine intervention into the lives of people just like you!

It's more than just a magazine—it's a ministry.

Shout! ...The dynamic magazine just for kids!

Shout! The Voice of Victory for Kids is a Bible-charged, action-packed, bimonthly magazine available FREE to kids everywhere! Featuring *Wichita Slim* and *Commander Kellie and the Superkids*, *Shout!* is filled with colorful adventure comics, challenging games and puzzles, exciting short stories, solve-it-yourself mysteries and much more!!

Stand up, sign up and get ready to *Shout!*

To receive a FREE subscription to
Believer's Voice of Victory,
or to give a child you know
a free subscription to *Shout!*
write or call:

Kenneth Copeland Ministries
Fort Worth, TX 76192-0001

Or call:
1-800-359-0075
(9 A.M. - 5 P.M. CT)

or log on to our website at:
www.kcm.org

World Offices
of Kenneth Copeland Ministries

For more information about KCM and a free
catalog, please write the office nearest you:

Kenneth Copeland Ministries
Fort Worth, TX 76192-0001

Kenneth Copeland
Locked Bag 2600
Mansfield Delivery Centre
QUEENSLAND 4122
AUSTRALIA

Kenneth Copeland
Post Office Box 15
BATH
BA1 1GD
ENGLAND U.K.

Kenneth Copeland
Private Bag X 909
FONTAINEBLEAU
2032
REPUBLIC OF SOUTH AFRICA

Kenneth Copeland
Post Office Box 378
Surrey
BRITISH COLUMBIA
V3T 5B6
CANADA

UKRAINE
L'VIV 290000
Post Office Box 84
Kenneth Copeland Ministries
L'VIV 290000
UKRAINE

The Harrison House Vision

Proclaiming the truth and the power
Of the Gospel of Jesus Christ
With excellence;

Challenging Christians to
Live victoriously,
Grow spiritually,
Know God intimately.